Jesus Is the Thesis

Jesus Is the Thesis

Meditations on a Christocentric Faith

Jeff Voth
Joshua Beck

WIPF & STOCK · Eugene, Oregon

JESUS IS THE THESIS
Meditations on a Christocentric Faith

Wipf & Stock
An Imprint of Wipf and Stock Publishers
199 W. 8th Ave., Suite 3
Eugene, OR 97401

www.wipfandstock.com

PAPERBACK ISBN: 978-1-6667-9406-9
HARDCOVER ISBN: 978-1-6667-9405-2
EBOOK ISBN: 978-1-6667-9404-5

SEPTEMBER 26, 2022 9:41 AM

To the Thesis.

JEFF

To my parents, who introduced me to the Thesis.

JOSHUA

Contents

Acknowledgments | vii

Introduction | 1

Part 1   The True Myth | 7

  1   Mythopoeia | 9

  2   Eucatastrophe | 16

  3   The Tao | 21

Part 2   Jesus in Every Book | 29

  4   The Fourth Man | 31

  5   That's My King! | 42

  6   Serpent Crusher | 51

Part 3   The Thesis Himself | 69

  7   The Kenotic King | 71

  8   For Our Sake | 82

  9   Resurrecting | 91

Part 4   Applying the Thesis | 99

  10   A Christocentric Ethic | 101

  11   A Christocentric Sexual Ethic | 109

  12   A Christocentric Political Ethic | 122

Conclusion | 131

Bibliography | 135

Acknowledgments

JESUS IS THE THESIS grew out of a course we co-teach at Oral Roberts University. We'd like to thank all the students who have participated in that course. You are a delight, and you helped shaped what is in these pages.

We are also grateful to Dr. Nathan French. Nathan worked extensively with Jeff, pouring through libraries to find ancient source materials, for chapter 3 especially. His time and expertise is greatly appreciated.

And finally, we need to thank Samantha Beck, Joshua's wife, who read through latter sections of the book to offer her always-impeccable critique. Her keen mind is unmatched.

Introduction

NEARLY NINE DECADES OLD, Polycarp was escorted into the stadium. He was the former bishop of Smyrna, now retired, and had been reported to the authorities as a follower of Christ. An odd ruling from Emperor Trajan forty years earlier brought this situation about. In response to one of his governors asking about these Christians, Trajan ruled that time should not be wasted seeking them out—but if accused and refuse to recant, they were to be punished.

Polycarp was accused. Now it was time to recant.

Several times he was asked to deny Christ and swear by the name of Caesar. Polycarp's response: "Eighty and six years have I served Him, and He never did me any injury; how then can I blaspheme my King and Savior?"[1] Polycarp was burned at the stake but not before offering a prayer to God in thanks, for judging him worthy to share in the suffering of Christ.[2]

To Polycarp, Jesus was not just a historical figure or moral teacher. He was real and present with him. Jesus was the one who gave him life and would reverse his coming death. Not only did Jesus offer him hope for life after his death but a path and purpose for his life before. Jesus was his Savior, but Jesus was also his King—the one he sought to follow, to obey, to have rule over him. For Polycarp's life, Jesus was the Thesis.

---

1. A. Roberts et al., "Encyclical Epistle," 41.

2. According to legend, the fire set to burn Polycarp miraculously avoided him, forming a circle around the pyre. When the officials realized they couldn't burn him, they had an executioner finish the job with a dagger. The blood that then poured out of Polycarp extinguished the flames, a sign reflecting the sacrifice of Christ that extinguishes the fires of hell.

The Apologists

Polycarp was a member of an important era in Christian history. The original followers of Jesus were dying off, and the church was attempting to establish itself as a legitimate religion. They were attacked from all sides—the Roman leaders, the followers of Greek philosophy, and the traditional Jews who didn't accept this new take on a messiah. Many of the attacks involved simple misunderstandings (i.e., the accusation that Christians were cannibals), but others were deeper and more complex.

Out of this reality came the first apologists. Those like Justin Martyr, Tertullian, Irenaeus, and Origen defended the Christian faith against those who sought to discredit it. They had to correct the misunderstandings, explain what the faith truly was, argue for its truth, and make the case that its truth was good for the lives of all people. Given the persecution of followers of Jesus, the task to establish Christianity as a credible religion was one with concrete and urgent consequences. Justin experienced this when he earned the moniker "Martyr" by being beheaded under the rule of Marcus Aurelius.[3]

One can easily see the need for apologetics at that time. The apologists' lives depended on a good defense of their faith. What about now? We no longer face this kind of persecution,[4] and we're certainly not the new kids in town. Many would argue that the time for apologetics, if there ever was one, is long in the past. The world's largest religion is no longer in need of defense. If anything, given the power it has acquired and the foul ways it has been used, the *modern* definition of apology is what needs to take place.

Although a strong one, that's not the only objection to contemporary apologetics. Others point to how apologists ignore the genuine complexity of issues, offering pat answers to difficult questions. Or how apologetics is used to belittle the other side, epitomized in the countless YouTube videos where an apologist "destroys" atheist arguments. Or how many apologetic methodologies fail to account for modern epistemology.

---

3. Gonzalez, *Early Church to Reformation*, 56. As noted earlier, the empire was not seeking out Christians but would try to execute them if accused. Interestingly, historical theologian Justo L. Gonzalez notes, "Justin had recently bested a famous pagan philosopher in a public debate, and there are indications that it was this philosopher who accused him."

4. This is not to ignore the real persecution that continues to happen in other parts of the world. See CT Editors, "50 Countries," for an overview as of Jan. 2021.

All of these are good reasons to ignore apologetics altogether. While it may have begun as a helpful way for persecuted Christians to address misunderstandings and establish their faith, it has in many ways become something different—something more sinister. Rather than bringing life to the weak, it has often turned into a weapon for the strong—the strong who are more concerned with winning than finding truth, more concerned with retaining power than living out a sacrificial faith, more concerned with doctrinal purity than the love of God and others.

We write these things while acknowledging that this is a work of apologetics. This is because, while we see the many flaws in the field of apologetics, we believe it still has a place. There are three reasons for this.

1. Apologetics is unavoidable.

We have come to recognize more and more, with the help of philosophers and cognitive scientists, that humans don't generally assess the reasons for an idea before choosing to accept it. We have a sense of what we believe, then account for the relevant facts based on those beliefs. While Aristotle considered humans the "rational animal," we are far more driven by emotion than we think. This fact tosses a wrench into the apologetic system, which assumes that if you give enough reasons for an idea, your opponent can't help but change their mind. This is especially true when thinking in terms of opponents—of winners and losers. If I'm going to "lose" by changing my mind, my fight-or-flight instinct will undoubtedly push me to keep that from happening.

Even so, this doesn't keep us from offering reasons for beliefs. To do that would be impossible, sacrificing an essential part of the human experience and sacrificing truth. We all have beliefs, and we offer reasons for those beliefs. Even those who claim apologetics is pointless or unhelpful offer reasons, or defenses, for their beliefs. At the most basic level, that is apologetics. A search for truth will always involve the offering and assessing of reasons.

Although considering this epistemic reality, we must enter conversations with the knowledge of our emotive life in mind. We need to recognize that people, including ourselves, aren't in search of reasons alone. We want beauty, good stories; we want to *want* to believe something. An apologetic that accounts for those realities is not somehow less intellectually rigorous but more so. It's a kind of rigor that accounts for the whole of human experience, making it more true to our God-given design.

2. Misunderstandings still need to be addressed.

While we are no longer in the early days, misunderstandings of the faith are still rampant—in the world and in the church itself. In the early church, confusion resulted from lack of knowledge. People didn't know what this faith was about, so rumors spread and needed to be addressed. Today, we have a different problem. Christianity is so ubiquitous, it has seeped into the surrounding culture, causing the lines between Christianity and culture to be blurred. In America, for example, everyone has heard of Christianity, but the Christianity they know of is one intimately associated with American values and particular political ideologies. The difficulty we face today is separating the essence of Christianity from its cultural milieu.

We believe the way of Jesus is not only good but essential for the flourishing of humanity. Because of that, we want to get his message right. That's not to say we have all the answers or that our way of understanding Jesus is right and everyone else is wrong. It's simply to say that we care—so taking part in the discussion is essential for all of us to come to a clearer picture of Jesus.

The best way for humans to come to true beliefs is by conversation. We don't reason well alone.[5] Apologetics is important because it is the act of engaging in the conversation. It goes wrong when that fact is forgotten, assuming the apologetic work is the debate's end, rather than the beginning.

3. Apologetics can be done well.

Apologetics doesn't have to be a hostile, us-versus-them, intellectual ego war. Jesus shows us how. He cares that people believe in him, so he gives them reasons to. He spends time correcting misunderstandings about his kingdom. Ultimately, though, his way of getting to people's hearts is by giving up his life. He doesn't seek power; he gives it up. Apologetics can be done well when it keeps its eyes on Jesus and embodies his way of life.

---

5. See Mercier and Sperber, *Enigma of Reason*—a helpful treatment on this epistemological dilemma.

One facet of this self-sacrificial approach is intellectual humility. Confidence in one's beliefs cannot preclude openness to the experience of others. When it does, that confidence shifts into blind certainty. At blind certainty, one has sacrificed truth on the altar of self. As finite beings, there will always be some new information to which to adjust our worldviews to fit, so a person searching for truth will have to always remain open to receiving it. When apologetics takes this humble approach, it can serve as a way for us to navigate this world of information, joining a community, all working to make the best of the knowledge we have.

A Thesis

If you think back on your middle school English class, you may remember learning about the thesis. The central statement in your paper, the main idea, the thought on which everything else holds together. Without that thesis, they told you, your essay will be aimless, without grounding.

Our argument in this book is that Jesus is the Thesis. He's the main idea, the one who holds everything together. He is the Thesis of our lives but also so much more. Our goal here is not to answer particular questions or defend against some heresy but to give a positive picture of the Christian faith. It's an attempt to address misunderstandings by pointing to the person himself, Jesus Christ. We believe that once that person has been encountered, everything else begins to make much more sense. As C. S. Lewis put it, "I believe in Christianity as I believe that the Sun has risen, not only because I see it, but because by it I see everything else."[6] Jesus is that Sun by which all of life is illuminated.

This work is a collaborative effort, both authors placing their stamp on every page. At the same time, we each take the lead in particular sections, letting our individual styles, and expertise, shine through.

With Jeff at the helm, we lay the foundations broadly, finding Jesus in story and Scripture. In part 1, we look at "The True Myth." Borrowing from J. R. R. Tolkien and C. S. Lewis, we assess how the myths humans have told and wished were true are made real in Christ. In addition, we argue that these myths and our human longings point to a universal morality found in the life and teachings of Jesus.

In part 2, we look at "Jesus in Every Book." Here, we argue that Jesus is the Thesis of Scripture. We search for him in every book, establish his

6. Lewis, *Weight of Glory*, 141.

centrality in all of Scripture, and then explore a particular example of this—from Genesis, the beginning. To make sense of the Bible, it is essential to understand this through line of Christ.

The pen then moves, so to speak, to Joshua's hand. In part 3, we look at "The Thesis Himself." Christians often talk about Christ "saving us" or "dying for our sins." We tease out what that means, as well as what it is missing, placing emphasis not only on Jesus's death but also on what his life and his resurrection mean for us.

And finally, in part 4, we look at "Applying the Thesis." We argue first for a Christocentric ethic, which we then apply to the areas of sexuality and politics. Through this, we hope to show the beauty of a life lived as a follower of Jesus.

We offer this work not as an end to the debate but the start of a conversation. It is our humble attempt to share with the world, with our students, with our friends, the beauty of Jesus Christ our King. He is the Thesis of the faith and, like Polycarp, of our lives.

Part 1

The True Myth

For light years and geological periods are mere arithmetic until the
shadow of man, the poet, the maker of myths, falls upon them.

—C. S. LEWIS, *MIRACLES*[1]

Myths and Makers of Myths

THE "MAKER OF MYTHS"? Who is he? He is the One who makes sense of the
grandest and truest telling of the story of humanity, by giving it language.
He gives context to the geological periods, mathematics, and science that
make up the facts of how the story works. In the above quote, Lewis eluci-
dates that through the vehicle of mythical fiction, context and vibrancy are
given to the brute facts. He held that in order to give context and life to the
facts, one needs imagination, and imagination was in fact given to man by
the most creative and imaginative One, God himself . . . the original Poet
and Storyteller. For he is the great Storyteller and Myth Maker, and he has
used men from time immemorial and in every culture to tell them the true
story. The story of his grand, pictorial, and imaginative effort to woo them
to himself.

---

1. Lewis, *Miracles*, 52–53.

1

Mythopoeia[1]

IT WAS J. R. R. TOLKIEN who first piqued C. S. Lewis's belief in Christianity by challenging him to consider it as the "true myth." Lewis's affirmative response came about when he (an avowed atheist at the time) and Tolkien were engaging in deep conversations about the power of myths. Lewis, in the heat of their intellectual battle on September 19, 1931, commented that myths were merely "lies breathed through silver,"[2] meaning that there was nothing true about them, albeit they were sometimes conveyed in beautiful and eloquent fashion. He would point to the *Aeneid*,[3] the *Epic of Gilgamesh*, Balder, Osiris, and other such mythologies and mythological figures as examples. In reaction to this statement, Tolkien went home and penned 148 lines of classic poetry that he entitled "Mythopoeia," or myth-maker. Beginning with these now famous words, "Philomythus [myth-lover] to Misomythus [myth-hater] aka Mythopoeia, by J. R. R. Tolkien, To one who said that myths were lies and therefore worthless, even though 'breathed

---

1. Mythopoeia is a term that can be first identified in the mid-nineteenth century and means the creation of and giving rise to myths. J. R. R. Tolkien popularized it with his poem of the same title written to his good friend C. S. Lewis in 1931. While Tolkien's work entitled "Mythopoeia" will not be provided in this work, the reader is encouraged to pause and read it in an effort to gain a fuller context; see Tolkien, *Tree and Leaf*.

2. Carpenter, *Inklings*, 42–45.

3. The *Aeneid* is one of many ancient examples pointing toward the understanding of the true myth that will be discussed. Throughout Christian history, from the church fathers to the present day, Virgil was/is seen as having been prophetic in some of his language, especially in his *Eclogues*. For a more detailed treatment of this issue, see Bourne, "Messianic Prophecy."

through silver."[4] The poem was instrumental in drawing Lewis toward belief in Christianity as truth. The discovery was so powerful an epiphany that only a month later Lewis would write on October 18, 1931, to his good friend Arthur Greeves:

> Now the story of Christ is simply a true myth: a myth working on us in the same way as the others, but with this tremendous difference that it really happened: and one must be content to accept it in the same way, remembering that it is God's myth where the others are men's myths: i.e. the Pagan stories are God expressing Himself through the minds of poets, using such images as He found there, while Christianity is God expressing Himself through what we call "real things." Therefore it is true.[5]

Over the years, Lewis would refine and restate his understanding of the true myth innumerable times and in varied forms. He does so beautifully and succinctly in an essay entitled "Myth Became Fact":

> The heart of Christianity is a myth which is also a fact. The old myth of the Dying God, without ceasing to be myth, comes down from the heaven of legend and imagination to the earth of history. It happens—at a particular date, in a particular place, followed by definable historical consequences. We pass from a Balder or an Osiris dying nobody knows when or where, to a historical person crucified (it is all in order) under Pontius Pilate. By becoming fact it does not cease to be myth: that is the miracle. I suspect that men have sometimes derived more spiritual sustenance from myths they did not believe than from the religion they professed. To be truly Christian we must both assent to the historical fact and also receive the myth (fact though it has become) with the same imaginative embrace which we accord to all myths. The one is hardly more important than the other.[6]

Lewis would ultimately settle at a place where he believed that myths, especially the true one, provided beneficial, eternal direction for the human condition. In his book *True Myth*, James Menzies asserts that:

> Lewis says that myth's universality points humanity in another direction, to something greater, to a personal, loving and eternal

4. Tolkien, *Tree and Leaf*, 83.

5. Lewis, *They Stand Together*, 427; letter dated Oct. 18, 1931.

6. Lewis, "Myth Became Fact," 63–67. This essay first appeared in *World Dominion* 22 (Sept.–Oct. 1944) 267–70.

"other." Myths serve as hints, clues, they are a suspicion that something more is going on than life under the sun . . . myth also helps people better understand the love of the triune God as well.[7]

Two books that would help Lewis refine his articulation of the true myth expressed by Christianity were *The Idea of the Holy*, by Ruldof Otto, and *The Everlasting Man*, by G. K. Chesterton. These works had so much impact upon him that they would make it onto his list of the ten books (other than the Bible) that had the greatest impact in shaping his vocational attitude and philosophy of life.[8] It will now be beneficial to have a brief overview of these two works, not only to understand more deeply their impact upon Lewis but to glean a deeper understanding of their place in the Christocentric focus of this book—that in fact, Jesus is the Thesis and the focal point of the true myth.

The Idea of the Holy

In all developed religions we find three strands or elements, and in
Christianity one more. The first of these is what Professor Otto calls
the experience of the Numinous.

—C. S. LEWIS, *THE PROBLEM OF PAIN*[9]

Rudolf Otto (1869–1937) was a German theologian, philosopher, and historian of religion. Otto is known worldwide for his work regarding man's experience of "the holy," *The Idea of the Holy* (1923) being his most important book. Otto became well known in his day for participating in Christian ecumenical activities, especially as they related to concerns between Christianity and other religions of the world (especially Judaism and Islam). This was due in great part to his conviction that there were three major commonalities in all developed religions. The first, and foundational of these commonalities, in Otto's opinion, was a term that he coined as the *numinous*. The numinous was a combination of the Latin *numen* (deity or religious power) and *omen* (a momentous sign).

---

7. Menzies, *True Myth*, 243.
8. For the list of the entire ten, see Voth, *Why Lewis?*, ch. 5, 41–58.
9. Lewis, *Problem of Pain*, 3.

The numinous was to be seen as an awe-inspiring element of religious experience. A holy presence that existed outside of humanity. A presence that held humans accountable to a particular morality, reminding them on a regular basis that they did not live rightly in accordance with that morality. However, Otto contended that Jesus was in fact the "one more" to which Lewis refers in the above quote. He was the ultimate personification of the numinous. John refers to it in John 1:1 when the "Word" (*logos*) became flesh; and Paul in Col 1:15–20 as Jesus was/is the One who holds "all things" together and ultimately makes all things right by going to the cross and resurrecting from the dead.

The apostles proclaim their Lord not only as "raised from the dead" but as "exalted" and "ascended" into heaven. That is in harmony with the picture of the universe that they shared with antiquity as a whole.[10]

Otto encourages Christians to use these understandings, pointing to Jesus as the numinous in human form, thereby engaging with adherents of other religions and helping them to see the whole truth, not merely the partial truth expressed in their religion. Otto's verbiage in *The Idea of the Holy* coupled with what Tolkien would later present as the "true myth" of Christianity would enlighten Lewis to an understanding of the centrality of Christ as the actual incarnation of the numinous—a fact that he believed set Christianity apart from any and every other religion.

The Everlasting Man

Have you tried Chesterton's *The Everlasting Man*? The best popular apologetic I know.[11]

For a good ("popular") defense of our position against modern waffle, to fall back on, I know nothing better than G. K. Chesterton's *The Everlasting Man*.[12]

—C. S. LEWIS

In *The Everlasting Man*, Lewis found for the first time a reasonable defense for the history of the world and the mythologies that existed in the great

10. Otto, *Idea of The Holy*, 227.

11. Lewis, quoted in Vanauken, *Severe Mercy*, 89–90.

12. Lewis, *Books, Broadcasts, and War*, 823.

civilizations. Written as a response to H. G. Wells's *The Outline of History*, it was a Christocentric, rational explanation for the existence, trajectory, and ultimate hope for mankind. The book's central theme asserts that when Christ steps onto the stage of history, the entire story begins to take shape and have context. Christ is, in fact, the extraordinary context that fulfills the yearning of mankind throughout history. His story was the one alluded to in the hieroglyphs of the cavemen, the actual personification and incarnation of all that the mythologies of men had hoped for. No ordinary man or fictitious figure was he:

> The populace had been wrong in many things, but they had not been wrong in believing that holy things could have a habitation and that divinity need not disdain the limits of time and space. And the barbarian who conceived the crudest fancy about the sun being stolen and hidden in a box, or the wildest myth about the god being rescued and his enemy being deceived with a stone, was nearer to the secret of the cave and knew more about the crisis of the world, than all those in the circle of cities round the Mediterranean who had become content with cold abstractions or cosmopolitan gesticulations; than all those who were spinning thinner and thinner threads of thought out of the transcendentalism of Plato or the orientalism of Pythagoras. The place that the shepherds found was not an academy or an abstract republic; it was not a place of myth and legends allegorized or dissected or explained away. It was a place of dreams come true.[13]

In Chesterton's mind, materialism was absurd and illogical in a myriad of ways. First, there was humanity's ability to reason. For him, human intelligence is unsurpassed in accomplishment and potentiality. Second, one must look only as far as early cave art to see that man has been drawing and painting since time immemorial. Other animals simply have not, cannot, nor will they ever be able to climb to the artistic heights and abilities of homo sapiens. Third, laughter is to be seen as something that distinguishes man from the beasts. It is a trait inherently placed in them as an *imago* of their Creator, who invariably laughs himself. Fourth, the religions, philosophies, and accompanying mythologies that have developed over the eons are undoubtedly best, and most fully satisfied, in the true Christian myth. These are only a few of the bricks laid in the foundation of his case against materialism; but ultimately, Chesterton posits that the more man is examined and compared to the animals, the less he actually looks like one and

---

13. Chesterton, *Everlasting Man*, 174–75.

that the person of Jesus Christ is undoubtedly the centrifugal force whereby all the dreams of humanity are set in motion—where all that is real and good and right make the most sense.

Eternity in Their Hearts

While the works of Tolkien, Lewis, Otto, and Chesterton provide a broad context for a Christocentric apologetic that has mythological, anthropological, philosophical, and theological tethering, in his book *Eternity in Their Hearts*, author and missiologist Don Richardson provides cohesive and comprehensive missiological understanding for these sentiments. Richardson has done a great amount of work to elucidate the presence of the true myth via an exposition of the common, comparable stories and prophecies existing in many cultures throughout the world. In fact, in his book he states emphatically:

> The primary thesis that I advocate in the book is a simple one: God's general revelation (see Ps. 19:1–4; Rom. 1:19–21; 2:14–15) is not an effete, inconsequential, inert bystander watching from the sidelines as God accomplishes everything related to redemption via special revelation alone. Instead, cosmic general revelation and canonized special revelation turn out to be stunningly coordinated players serving on the same team. God, via general revelation, imprints human cultures in a variety of ways. Discerning the way God has already imprinted a given culture helps a missionary discover how to poignantly explain redemption to members of that culture.[14]

Richardson's work provides a biblical, ethnological, and anthropological synthesis for the true myth, with the possibility of leveraging its sometimes obvious, sometimes more covert presence for the furtherance of the gospel. He asserts that embedded into many cultures are found stories, pictures, glimpses, and sometimes blatantly overt references to a good, loving, and redemptive Creator. A Creator that looks, acts, and reaches for all people like the God of the Bible. The Father of Jesus.

From the prophetic utterances of Epimenides in the sixth century BC that would ultimately prepare the way for the apostle Paul to speak with those worshiping an "unknown god" in Acts 17, to the Canaanites, the Incas of South America, the Santal of India, the Gedeo of Ethiopia, and the

---

14. Richardson, *Eternity in Their Hearts*, 190.

Mbaka of the Central African Republic, Richardson asserts emphatically that the God of Abraham, the Father of Jesus, has prepared all people to receive his gospel, good news in the midst of the chaos and catastrophe, by setting "eternity in the hearts of men" (Eccl 3:11 NIV).

This chapter has established that mythopoeic yearnings, set in the hearts of men by their Creator, have been expressed through the millennia in many and varied forms. We will now turn once again to the great storyteller himself, J. R. R. Tolkien, to help give insight to the nature of those stories and how they might be used to tell the most important, grandest, and redemptive story of all.

2

Eucatastrophe

But the "consolation" of fairytales has another aspect than the imaginative satisfaction of ancient desires. Far more important is the Consolation of the Happy Ending. Almost I would venture to assert that all complete fairystories must have it.

—J. R. R. TOLKIEN, "ON FAIRY STORIES"[1]

WHAT HAS ALREADY BEEN referred to in this section as men's myths, the numinous (Otto), cave art (Chesterton), or God's imprinting (Richardson), Tolkien refers to in a literary context as "fairystories." In his essay "On Fairy Stories," he would invent a term that expressed what he felt rested at the very center of a complete understanding of the true myth:

> I will call it, Eucatastrophe. The eucatastrophic tale is the true form of fairytale, and its highest function. . . . The Birth of Christ is the eucatastrophe of Man's history. The Resurrection is the eucatastrophe of the story of the Incarnation. This story begins and ends in joy. It has preeminently the "Inner consistency of reality." There is no tale ever told that men would rather find was true, and none which so many sceptical men have accepted as true on its own merit. For the Art of it has the supremely convincing tone of Primary Art, that is, of Creation. To reject it leads either to sadness or to wrath.[2]

1. Tolkien, "On Fairy Stories," 22.
2. Tolkien, "On Fairy Stories," 22.

For Tolkien, the euchatastrophe is the opposite of catastrophe. Catastrophe is that which is often regarded as the downturn of a story. The place where all hope seems to have been lost. That place where the story shifts for the good is where eucatastrophe is to be found. In Tolkien's words, it's "the sudden joyous turn."[3] It's there, when circumstances can't get much bleaker, that hope emerges. For him, the Christian story contained in the Gospels is the most powerful literary exposition of the true myth and its eucatastrophic redeeming power:

> It has long been my feeling (a joyous feeling) that God redeemed the corrupt making creatures, men, in a way fitting to this aspect, as to others, of their strange nature. The Gospels contain a fairy story, or a story of a larger kind, which embraces all the essence of fairystories. They contain many marvels—peculiarly artistic, beautiful, and moving, "mythical" in their perfect, self-contained significance; and among the marvels is the greatest and most complete and conceivable eucatastrophe. But this story has entered human history.[4]

In his book *Epic: The Story God is Telling*, John Eldredge heartily agrees with Tolkien and affirms that really all the great stories "pretty much follow the same story line."[5] Things are good while life rolls along quite nicely; then catastrophe appears. Sickness, tragic occurrences, or some combination of events lead to a dangerous, mysterious, and difficult epic journey. Then, at just the right moment, which feels like it's almost too late, the hero appears and sets things right. Life is good again. The realized hope of happily-ever-after has arrived:

> It's true of every fairy tale, every myth, every western, every epic—just about every story you can think of, one way or another. *Braveheart*, *Titanic*, and the *Star Wars* series, *Gladiator*, *The Lord of the Rings* trilogy. They pretty much all follow the same story line. Have you ever wondered why? Every story, great and small, shares the same essential structure, because every story we tell borrows its power from a *Larger Story*, a *Story* woven into the fabric of our being—what pioneer psychologist Carl Jung tried to explain as archetype, or what his more recent popularizer Joseph Campbell called myth.[6] All of these stories borrow from *the* Story.

3. Tolkien, *Tolkien on Fairy-Stories*, 75.

4. Tolkien, "On Fairy Stories," 23.

5. Eldredge, *Epic*, 12.

6. For an in-depth exploration of this subject, see Menzies, *True Myth*. Menzies

From Reality. We hear echoes of it through our lives. . . . There is a Story written on the human heart. 'He has planted eternity in the human heart (Eccl. 3:11)'.[7]

Yes, the mythopoeic, eucatastrophic hope in all men is not some expression of mere Freudian wish fulfillment; it has been woven by the Creator into the tapestry of human design and culture since the beginning. But the telling of the story to which Eldredge refers is remarkably unique. Unique in the incarnational presence of suffering, which lies at the core of this epic tale.

The Suffering God

Apologist Tim Keller sees the eucatastrophic story referred to by Tolkien and Eldredge in the previous quotes as a story that is, in fact, redemptively tragic. Unique in history in that the suffering portrayed is personified by a deity who becomes human, then suffers on behalf of and with those humans as they are imperiled on an epic journey. Redemptively tragic and holistically incarnational is this tale. In his book entitled *King's Cross*, Keller asserts that eucatastrophe is really what all people long for but what many moderns and postmoderns totally miss. Miss, because they have been blinded and desensitized by the cultural hubris that accompanies empiricism, relativism, and hedonism. The dark, lonely, oft misunderstood place of suffering does not seem to warrant much of a popular response. Suffering that is sometimes self-induced, sometimes inexplicable. Keller asserts that the story of Jesus can potentially bring eucatastrophic beauty into the darkness of the age, because he suffers with humanity . . . for humanity:

> Christianity is the only religious faith that says that God Himself actually suffered, actually cried out in suffering. Now what good is that? To Jesus's followers assembled at the cross, it certainly seemed senseless: that there was no good in it at all. But in fact, they came to realize that Jesus's suffering was of immense good to them, as can we. Why? Because they would eventually see that

---

compares and contrasts C. S. Lewis's position regarding myth with that of Joseph Campbell. He concludes that while Campbell's work was valuable in its establishment of the presence and power of myth, he fell far short of Lewis's understanding that the personal God of the Bible put a desire in man's heart to use myth to draw all men to himself (see Eccl 3:11).

7. Eldredge, *Epic*, 13.

they had been looking right at the greatest act of God's love, power and justice in history. God came into the world and suffered and died on the cross in order to save us. It is the ultimate proof of His love for us. And when you suffer, you may be completely in the dark about the reason for your own suffering. . . . The cross proves that He loves you and understands what it means to suffer. It also demonstrates that God can be working in your life even when it seems like there is no rhyme or reason to what is happening.[8]

Yes, the true myth is expressed initially, shockingly in the face of the suffering God screaming in agony on the cross. However, the cataclysmic force of it is most fully expressed in the fact that he did not stay impaled in that agonizing place. Had he remained there, ultimately entombed to rot and decay, as is the fate of every other corpse, the mythical story would be totally different, ending in a cave of death. But that is not what occurred. The true myth doesn't conclude with a catastrophe, forever encased in a grave of suffering. It provides a door to a place of joy and eternal hope— something more than just hopeful storytelling. It is an eternal extension of the narrative of hope into a hopeless world. It is a means of smuggling joy past what Lewis would refer to as the "watchful dragons"[9] that endeavor to use whatever means necessary to snuff out the kindled sparks of an eternal hope. It is a bloodstained hope that spawns more hope—the hope of living happily ever after with the resurrected Hope himself.

The Playwright

In response to those who might question the reality of God's existence and the validity of Jesus Christ being the eucatastrophic focal point of history and man's myths, Keller, in his book *The Reason For God*, offers a powerful metaphor as a means of explanation. He proposes that God is not some force or object to be empirically poked at, prodded, or measured. Rather, he is more like a playwright—one who relates to the characters in a play that he has written. Human beings, the characters in the play, might be able to know about the Playwright but only as much as he chooses to reveal about himself in the body of his play. It would be impossible to know the Playwright exhaustively by watching, reading, or experiencing the play. Yes, some things might be known—but not all things. Ultimately, the

8. Keller, *King's Cross*, 208–9.
9. Lewis, *Of Other Worlds*, 37.

Playwright can be known only by what he has chosen to personally reveal about himself:

> If there is a God, we characters in his play have to hope that he put some information about himself in the play. But Christians believe that he did more than give us information. He wrote himself into the play as the main character in history, when Jesus was born in a manger and rose from the dead. He is the one with whom we have to do.[10]

Eldredge adds to these sentiments, summing it up quite nicely as he affirms in holistic fashion that:

> God has set eternity in our hearts. We've been trying to express it in the stories that we tell. Or rather, it has been trying to express itself, this eternity written on our hearts. And, the Scripture bears witness that, in fact, the best of these stories are very close indeed to what is about to happen in our Story . . . it will take your breath away . . . 'Then I saw a new heaven and a new earth (Revelation 21:1).'[11]

If the Creator/Playwright/suffering God has placed into his created beings the desire to tell stories that ultimately all point to the one true story—his story—one would expect lifestyle ramifications and moral codes to be included in such stories; elements of right and wrong, good and evil; and the accompanying codes of conduct associated with those who live such lives. We will now endeavor to find historical evidence of such codes.

10. Keller, *Reason for God*, 128.
11. Eldredge, *Epic*, 80–81.

3

The Tao

The idea of collecting independent testimonies presupposes that "civilizations" have arisen in the world independently of one another; or even that humanity has had several independent emergences on this planet. The biology and anthropology involved in such an assumption are extremely doubtful. It is by no means certain that there has ever (in the sense required) been more than one civilization in all history. It is at least arguable that every civilization we find has been derived from another civilization and, in the last resort, from a single centre—"carried" like an infectious disease or like the Apostolical succession.[1]

—C. S. LEWIS, *THE ABOLITION OF MAN*

IN THE ABOVE QUOTE, C. S. Lewis makes a bold assertion in the appendix to his book *The Abolition of Man*. While the thesis in *Abolition* doesn't speak directly of the "true myth" per se, he does assert that many cultures throughout the world, since time immemorial, come "from a single centre," thus possessing comparable elements of their cosmologies and comparable value systems pertaining to ethics and morality. This is especially true in some of the oldest cultures. Common and comparable themes and values exist in Sumerian, Egyptian, Babylonian, Persian, Chinese, Norse, and Judeo-Christian mythologies and creeds. These commonalities are labeled by Lewis as Natural Law, or the Law. In noting these things, Lewis attempts

---

1. Lewis, *Abolition of Man*, 83–84.

to make a case for the presence of a universal morality that could summarily point to one primary morality—one that has been conveyed to humanity through stories, myths, legends, and creeds.

To make his case, he borrows a term from the Far East, called the *Tao*.[2] *Tao* literally means "the way." Lewis explains thusly:

> The Chinese speak of a great thing (the greatest thing) called the Tao. It is the reality beyond all predicates. . . . It is Nature, it is the Way, the Road. It is the Way in which the universe goes on, the way in which things everlastingly emerge, stilly and tranquilly, into space and time. It is also the Way which every man should tread in imitation of that cosmic and super cosmic progression, confirming all activities to the great exemplar. . . . The ancient Jews likewise praise the Law as being true.[3]

Lewis purposefully chose a non-Western, inclusive term to propose that there might in fact be a universal moral code present in many (if not all) cultures. A way that exemplifies the best and most proper way to live. A way that all peoples are inherently supposed to know. The way of obedience. An obedience that initially played out in the story of one God and his people, the Jews. Nevertheless, a story that echoes and reverberates through and into many other cultures at least partially and in some more so than others. This, Lewis believes, accounts for the fact that there are many common themes regarding best practices towards living the good life and for treating one another properly. This way would be the way to which the apostle Paul emphatically points from a Judeo-Christian perspective as he states:

> For what can be known about God is plain to them, because God has shown it to them. [20] Ever since the creation of the world his eternal power and divine nature, invisible though they are, have been understood and seen through the things he has made. So they are without excuse. (Rom 1:19–20)

The way and its accompanying practices are referred to in the appendix of *The Abolition of Man* as laws and duties; eight are identified. In this chapter, each of these practices will be examined, with accompanying

---

2. It is important to note that in using the term *Tao*, Lewis is not asserting that the values of which he speaks are necessarily Taoist or refer to Taoism in a religious sense. He uses the term as a descriptor for a universal morality that potentially points towards a universal story and mythology.

3. Lewis, *Abolition of Man*, 83.

examples from three ancient cultures and a final assertion from Judeo-Christian history as expressed in the Bible. To view these statements in the same context is quite compelling.

1. *The Law of General Beneficence*: The presence of an inherent moral obligation to act for others' benefit, by helping them to further their own personal and legitimate interests. Often, this entails removing or preventing possible harms. It is referred to as general because it is in reference to, for, and towards *all* persons. Lewis cites the following:[4]

   - "I have not slain men." (ancient Egyptian)

   - "Who meditates oppression, his dwelling is overturned." (Babylonian)

   - "In Nástrond (= Hell) I saw . . . murderers." (Old Norse)

   - "You shall not murder." (Judeo-Christian)[5]

2. *The Law of Special Beneficence*: The presence of an inherent moral obligation to act for others' benefit but more specific and personal to the individual.

   - "Natural affection is a thing right and according to Nature." (ancient Greek)

   - "Nothing can ever change the claims of kinship for a right-thinking man." (Anglo-Saxon)

   - "Is it only the sons of Atreus who love their wives? For every good man, who is right minded, loves and cherishes his own." (ancient Greek)

---

4. Lewis, *Abolition of Man*, 83–84.

5. Lewis provides an in-text citation for each of these references in the appendix. We are providing a fuller citation here for the benefit of our reader. For ancient Egyptian reference, see Alan Gardiner, "Ethics and Morality (Egyptian)," in Hastings et al., *Encyclopaedia of Religion and Ethics*, 5:481; for Babylonian ("Hymn to Shamash"), see A. Jeremias, "Ethics and Morality (Babylonian)," in Hastings et al., *Encyclopaedia of Religion and Ethics*, 5:445; for Old Norse (*Völuspá*), see Bray, *Elder or Poetic Edda*, 286–87 (lines 38–39); for Judeo-Christian, see Exod 20:13 KJV. (It is unclear which reference text Lewis used to cite the *Völuspá* poem. However, we are citing a 1908 publication of the original Old Norse with an English translation for easy access.)

- "And whoever does not provide for relatives, and especially for family members, has denied the faith and is worse than an unbeliever." (Judeo-Christian)[6]

3. *Duties to Parents, Elders, Ancestors*: The understanding that there are inherently good and proper ways to act regarding one's parents and the elderly.

- "Your father is an image of the Lord of Creation, your mother an image of the Earth. For him who fails to honor them, every work of piety is in vain. This is the first duty." (Hindu)
- "Has he despised Father and Mother?" (Babylonian)
- "When proper respect of the dead is shown at the end and continued after they are far away, the moral force (*te*) of a people has reached the highest point." (ancient Chinese)
- "Honor your father and your mother, so that your days may be long in the land that the Lord your God is giving you." (Judeo-Christian)[7]

4. *Duties to Children and Posterity (future generations)*: The understanding that there are inherently good and proper ways to treat children and future generations.

- "Children, the old and the poor, etc. should be considered as lords of the atmosphere." (Hindu)
- "To marry and to beget children." (ancient Greek)
- "Great reverence is owed to a child." (Roman)
- "Then little children were being brought to him in order that he might lay his hands on them and pray. The disciples spoke sternly to those who brought them; but Jesus said, 'Let the little children come to me, and do not stop them; for it is to such as these that the

---

6. For first ancient Greek reference, see Epictetus, *Epictetus*, 1:83 (bk 1, ch. 11); for Anglo-Saxon, see Heaney, *Beowulf*, 65 (line 2600); for second ancient Greek, see Homer, *Iliad*, 31 (bk 9, line 340); for Judeo-Christian, see 1 Tim 5:8 KJV.

7. Lewis here provides his translation of Paul Janet's own French translation of the Hindu *Laws of Manu*; see Janet, *Histoire*, 9. For Babylonian reference (*List of Sins*), see A. Jeremias, "Ethics and Morality (Babylonian)," in Hastings et al., *Encyclopaedia of Religion and Ethics*, 5:446; for ancient Chinese, see Confucius, *Analects of Confucius*, 85 (bk 1, saying 9); for Judeo-Christian, see Exod 20:12 KJV.

kingdom of heaven belongs.' And he laid his hands on them and went on his way." (Judeo-Christian)[8]

5. *The Law of Justice*: The presence of an inherent moral obligation to treat others fairly in sexual, social, criminal, and restorative contexts.

- "Has he approached his neighbor's wife?" (Babylonian)
- "I saw in Nastrond (=Hell) . . . beguilers of others' wives." (Old Norse)
- "I have not stolen." (ancient Egyptian)
- "Regard him whom thou knowest like him whom thou knowest not." (ancient Egyptian)
- "Thou shalt not commit adultery." (Judeo-Christian)
- "Thou shalt not bear false witness against thy neighbor." (Judeo-Christian)[9]

6. *The Law of Good Faith and Veracity (truthfulness)*: The presence of an inherent moral obligation to speak and act truthfully.

- "A sacrifice is obliterated by a lie and the merit of alms by an act of fraud." (Hindu)
- "With his mouth was he full of Yea, in his heart full of Nay?" (Babylonian)
- "[The gentleman] must learn to be faithful to his superiors and to keep promises." (ancient Chinese)
- "Let your word be 'Yes, Yes' or 'No, No'; anything more than this comes from the evil one." (Judeo-Christian)[10]

8. For Hindu reference, see Janet, *Histoire*, 1:8; for ancient Greek, Lewis's reference was unclear, though a similar statement appears in Epictetus, *Epictetus*, 1:79; for Roman, see pt. 4, satires 12–14, in Juvenal, *Juvenal*, 101; for Judeo-Christian, see Matt 19:13–15 KJV.

9. For Babylonian reference, see A. Jeremias, "Ethics and Morality (Babylonian)," in Hastings et al., *Encyclopaedia of Religion and Ethics*, 5:446; for Old Norse (*Völuspá*), see Bray, *Elder or Poetic Edda*, 286–87 (lines 38–39); for ancient Egyptian (*Confession of the Righteous Soul*), see Alan Gardiner, "Ethics and Morality (Egyptian)," in Hastings et al., *Encyclopaedia of Religion and Ethics*, 5:478 and 481; for Judeo-Christian, see Exod 20:14, 16 KJV.

10. For Hindu reference (*Laws of Manu*), see Janet, *Histoire*, 1:6; for Babylonian ("Hymn to Shamash"), see A. Jeremias, "Ethics and Morality (Babylonian)," in Hastings

7. *The Law of Mercy*: The presence of an inherent moral obligation to extend kindness, forgiveness, and love towards someone who is undeserving and/or unable to repay the kindness.

- "The poor and the sick should be regarded as lords of the atmosphere." (Hindu)

- "Whoso makes intercession for the weak, well pleasing is this to Shamash." (Babylonian)

- "There, Thor, you got disgrace, when you beat women." (Old Norse)

- "Then he will answer them, 'Truly I tell you, just as you did not do it to one of the least of these, you did not do it to me.'" (Judeo-Christian)[11]

8. *The Law of Magnanimity (big in spirit)*: The presence of an inherent moral obligation to act greatly in mind and heart, even at one's own peril. To be courageous and honorable. It usually encompasses a disdain for petty and cowardly activities.

- "There are two kinds of injustice: the first is found in those who do an injury, the second in those who fail to protect another from injury when they can." (Roman)

- "To take no notice of a violent attack is to strengthen the heart of the enemy. Vigor is valiant, but cowardice is vile." (ancient Egyptian)

- "Death is better for every man than life with shame." (Anglo-Saxon)

- "Very truly, I tell you, unless a grain of wheat falls into the earth and dies, it remains just a single grain; but if it dies, it bears much fruit. Those who love their life lose it, and those who hate their life in this world will keep it for eternal life." (Judeo-Christian)[12]

---

et al., *Encyclopaedia of Religion and Ethics*, 5:445; for ancient Chinese, see Confucius, *Analects*, 85 (bk 1, saying 8); for Judeo-Christian, see Matt 5:37 KJV.

11. For Hindu reference, see Janet, *Histoire*, 1:8; for Babylonian ("Hymn to Shamash"). see A. Jeremias, "Ethics and Morality (Babylonian)," in Hastings et al., *Encyclopaedia of Religion and Ethics*, 5:445; for Old Norse ("The Lay of Hárbarðr"), see Bray, *Elder or Poetic Edda*, v. 38, pp. 194–95; for Judeo-Christian, see Matt 25:45 KJV.

12. For Roman reference, see Cicero, *Ethical Writings*, 14–15 (bk 1, saying 7); for ancient Egyptian (Pharoah Senusert III), see Hall, *Ancient History*, 161; for Anglo-Saxon, see Heaney, *Beowulf*, 72, v. 2890; for Judeo-Christian, see John 12:24–25 KJV.

Through the examination of mythopoeia, eucatastrophe, and the stories, creeds, and cosmologies referred to in the Tao, an effort has been made to establish that throughout the eons of time, humans have endeavored to live properly and correctly. Some have lived better, more productively and beneficently, than others, but most have tried to live out something close to, or in actual accordance with the "single centre" spoken of in the first paragraph of this chapter. While they are all, in some form or fashion, expressions of the true myth, Lewis's assertion, as well as Richardson's earlier, is that the Judeo-Christian way is the most correct and accurate explanation of the Way—an assertion that rests upon the fact that there was One who was a Jew and lived the way perfectly. That One was Jesus Christ. He would refer to himself as the Way, the Truth, and the Life (John 14:6). He actually claimed to be the Tao. A bold and exclusive claim it was—a claim bolstered by his prediction that he would live the perfect and sinless life, die, then resurrect—a resurrection that would give him the right to die sacrificially and resurrect victoriously for anyone who would submit their lives to him. He was the consummation and vivification of everything that comprised and pointed to the true myth—the single and perfect deified "centre" in human form.

Lewis summarizes the effects of these assertions quite nicely in the following quote from *Mere Christianity*:

> If you are a Christian you do not have to believe that all the other religions are simply wrong all through. If you are an atheist you do have to believe that the main point in all the religions of the whole world is simply one huge mistake. If you are a Christian, you are free to think that all those religions, even the queerest ones, contain at least some hint of the truth . . . of course, being a Christian does mean thinking that where Christianity differs from other religions, Christianity is right, and they are wrong. As in arithmetic—there is only one right answer to a sum, and all other answers are wrong; but some of the wrong answers are much nearer being right than others.[13]

Christianity is exactly and perfectly right because the answer to the sum is Jesus. All Jesus. He is the foundation and the Thesis for *all* that is right, true, and good. He is in and of himself the best life. It now behooves us to survey the Scriptures that tell his epic, mythological, true story.

13. Lewis, *Mere Christianity*, 35.

PART 1 | THE TRUE MYTH

Part 2

Jesus in Every Book

The center and circumference of the Christian life is none other than the person of Christ. All other things, including those related to him, are eclipsed by the sight of His peerless worth. God put an image in our galaxy to demonstrate what Christ is to us. We call it the sun. Without it, no life can exist on planet Earth. We are dependent upon the sun for everything. And just as the sun is the center of our solar system, Jesus Christ is the centerpiece of God's universe, and even our lives. "To you who fear My name the Sun of Righteousness will arise with healing in His wings" (Mal. 4:2).

—LEONARD SWEET & FRANK VIOLA, *JESUS MANIFESTO*[1]

THE CENTERPIECE AND THESIS to the true myth is none other than Jesus. In this section we will delve deeply into the essence of this understanding. As we do, we will become adept at seeing him overtly, metaphorically, positionally, and often as a combination of one or more of these aspects of his nature. Picture upon picture of his nature and personhood. When seen and received as the center of the entire canon of Scripture and the lens through which truth, reality, and goodness are to be viewed, purpose is breathed into human existence. Purpose that pulsates through generations and geographies. Purpose that lives in, moves with, and mysteriously and miraculously changes altogether the nature of man's being.

1. Sweet and Viola, *Jesus Manifesto*, 1.

4

The Fourth Man

WHILE HE WAS CERTAINLY not the first preacher to focus upon the identity of a mysterious figure described in Dan 3:1–30,[1] in arguably his most famous sermon, entitled "The Fourth Man," legendary evangelist Oral Roberts would be one of the most renowned of his time to do so.[2] Initially, his sermon would focus upon the capital offense of three young Hebrew men who had been thrown into a fiery furnace. Refusing to kowtow to popular culture and bow in worshipful homage to King Nebuchadnezzar, their death was a certainty. Roberts would note however, that after having thrown the three into the furnace (3:24), the king and audience witnessing the execution saw four individuals walking around rather comfortably in the flames. One whom they said looked like "a son of the gods" (Dan 3:25).

"Who was that fourth man?" Roberts would rhetorically ask his hearers.

Then, staring into their eyes, with fire in his, he would emphatically answer by giving sixty-six responses—one for each book of the Bible. Providing example after example after example as to the identity of the mysterious fourth man. With types, names, pictures, phrases, and images, he would make his case—a case that would ultimately crescendo in Jesus. Jesus was undoubtedly and irrefutably the Fourth Man. He was and is the Thesis of the entirety of Scripture. He is the ultimate picture painted by every book. He is heaven's great masterpiece. Millions of hearers would be blessed

---

1. The reader is encouraged to stop and read these verses from Daniel to give the content in this chapter a fuller context.

2. See O. Roberts, "Fourth Man," unnumbered pages, for the following descriptions and quotes.

by this sermon so many years ago; yet it still resonates fresh and vibrant. Be challenged to engage with this historic word, by reading the next few pages out loud. Read it. Hear it. Ingest and imbibe. Wonder at the vastness. Bask in the goodness. Be comforted by the greatness that is Jesus as you answer the question *Who is that fourth man?*

In Genesis (3:15) he is the *Seed of the Woman*:

> And I will put enmity between you and the woman, and between your seed and her Seed; He shall bruise your head, and you shall bruise His heel.[3]

In Exodus (12:6–7) he is the *Passover Lamb*:

> Now you shall keep it until the fourteenth day of the same month. Then the whole assembly of the congregation of Israel shall kill it at twilight. [7] And they shall take some of the blood and put it on the two doorposts and on the lintel of the houses where they eat it.

In Leviticus (4:5–7) he is the *High Priest*:

> Then the anointed priest shall take some of the bull's blood and bring it to the tabernacle of meeting. [6] The priest shall dip his finger in the blood and sprinkle some of the blood seven times before the LORD, in front of the veil of the sanctuary. [7] And the priest shall put some of the blood on the horns of the altar of sweet incense before the LORD, which is in the tabernacle of meeting; and he shall pour the remaining blood of the bull at the base of the altar of the burnt offering, which is at the door of the tabernacle of meeting.

In Numbers (9:15–16) he is the *Cloud by Day and the Fire by Night*:

> Now on the day that the tabernacle was raised up, the cloud covered the tabernacle, the tent of the Testimony; from evening until morning it was above the tabernacle like the appearance of fire. [16] So it was always: the cloud covered it by day, and the appearance of fire by night."

In Deuteronomy (18:15–19) he is the *Prophet like Moses*:

> The LORD your God will raise up for you a Prophet like me from your midst, from your brethren. Him you shall hear, [16] according to all you desired of the LORD your God in Horeb in the day of the assembly, saying, "Let me not hear again the voice of the LORD my

---

3. All Scripture references in this chapter are from the NKJV unless otherwise noted.

God, nor let me see this great fire anymore, lest I die." [17] And the LORD said to me: "What they have spoken is good. [18] I will raise up for them a Prophet like you from among their brethren, and will put My words in His mouth, and He shall speak to them all that I command him. [19] And it shall be that whoever will not hear My words, which He speaks in My name, I will require it of him."

In Joshua (6:2–5) he is the *Captain of Salvation*:

And the LORD said to Joshua: "See! I have given Jericho into your hand, its king, and the mighty men of valor. 3 You shall march around the city, all you men of war; you shall go all around the city once. This you shall do six days. [4] And seven priests shall bear seven trumpets of rams' horns before the ark. But the seventh day you shall march around the city seven times, and the priests shall blow the trumpets. [5] It shall come to pass, when they make a long blast with the ram's horn, and when you hear the sound of the trumpet, that all the people shall shout with a great shout; then the wall of the city will fall down flat. And the people shall go up every man straight before him."

In Judges (1:1–2) he is the *Judge and Lawgiver*:

Now after the death of Joshua it came to pass that the children of Israel asked the LORD, saying, "Who shall be first to go up for us against the Canaanites to fight against them?"

[2] And the LORD said, "Judah shall go up. Indeed I have delivered the land into his hand."

In Ruth (3:8–9) he is the *Kinsman Redeemer*:

At midnight the man was startled and turned over, and behold, a woman lay at his feet! [9] He said, "Who are you?" And she answered, "I am Ruth, your servant. Spread your wings over your servant, for you are a redeemer." (ESV)

In First and Second Samuel (1 Sam 1:26–28) he is the *Trusted Prophet*:

And she said, "O my lord! As your soul lives, my lord, I am the woman who stood by you here, praying to the LORD. [27] For this child I prayed, and the LORD has granted me my petition which I asked of Him. [28] Therefore I also have lent him to the LORD; as long as he lives he shall be lent to the LORD." So they worshiped the LORD there.

In the books of Kings (1 Kgs 3:3) and Chronicles he is the *Reigning King*:

> And the LORD said to him: "I have heard your prayer and your supplication that you have made before Me; I have consecrated this house which you have built to put My name there forever, and My eyes and My heart will be there perpetually."

In Ezra (7:6, 9b, 10) he is the *Faithful Scribe*:

> This Ezra came up from Babylon; and he was a skilled scribe in the Law of Moses, which the LORD God of Israel had given. The king granted him all his request, according to the hand of the LORD his God upon him. . . . ⁹ According to the good hand of his God upon him. ¹⁰ For Ezra had prepared his heart to seek the Law of the LORD, and to do it, and to teach statutes and ordinances in Israel.

In Nehemiah (2:4–5) he is the *Rebuilder of the Broken-Down Walls of Human Life*:

> Then the king said to me, "What do you request?" So I prayed to the God of heaven. ⁵ And I said to the king, "If it pleases the king, and if your servant has found favor in your sight, I ask that you send me to Judah, to the city of my fathers' tombs, that I may rebuild it."

In Esther (2:22) he is *Mordecai*:

> So the matter became known to Mordecai, who told Queen Esther, and Esther informed the king in Mordecai's name.

In Job (42:10a, 12a) he is the *Dayspring on High and the Ever-Living Redeemer*:

> And the LORD restored Job's losses when he prayed for his friends. Indeed the LORD gave Job twice as much as he had before. . . . ¹² Now the LORD blessed the latter days of Job more than his beginning.

In the Psalms (23:1) he is the *Lord Our Shepherd*:

> The LORD is my shepherd; I shall not want.

In Proverbs (8:14–17) and Ecclesiastes (12:9–11) he is the *Wisdom of God*:

Counsel is mine, and sound wisdom; I am understanding, I have strength. [15] By me kings reign, and rulers decree justice. [16] By me princes rule, and nobles, all the judges of the earth. [17] I love those who love me, and those who seek me diligently will find me. (Prov)

And moreover, because the Preacher was wise, he still taught the people knowledge; yes, he pondered and sought out and set in order many proverbs. [10] The Preacher sought to find acceptable words; and what was written was upright—words of truth. [11] The words of the wise are like goads, and the words of scholars are like well-driven nails, given by one Shepherd. (Eccl)

In the Song of Songs (2:16) he is the *Lover and the Bridegroom*:

My beloved *is* mine, and I *am* his. He feeds *his flock* among the lilies.

In Isaiah (9:6) he is the *Prince of Peace*:

For unto us a Child is born, unto us a Son is given; And the government will be upon His shoulder. And His name will be called Wonderful, Counselor, Mighty God, Everlasting Father, Prince of Peace.

In Jeremiah (23:5) he is the *Righteous Branch*:

"Behold, the days are coming," says the LORD, "That I will raise to David a Branch of righteousness; a King shall reign and prosper and execute judgment and righteousness in the earth."

In Lamentations (3:19–23) he is the *Weeping Prophet*:

I remember my affliction and my wandering, the bitterness and the gall. [20] I well remember them, and my soul is downcast within me. [21] Yet this I call to mind and therefore I have hope: [23] Because of the LORD's great love we are not consumed, for his compassions never fail. [24] They are new every morning; great is your faithfulness.

In Ezekiel (10:14–15) he is the *Four-Faced Man*:

Each one had four faces: the first face was the face of a cherub, the second face the face of a man, the third the face of a lion, and the fourth the face of an eagle. [15] And the cherubim were lifted up. This was the living creature I saw by the River Chebar.

In Daniel (3:25) he is the *Fourth Man*:

"Look!" he answered, "I see four men loose, walking in the midst of the fire; and they are not hurt, and the form of the fourth is like the Son of God."

In Hosea (3:2–3) he is the *Faithful Husband*:

So I bought her for myself for fifteen shekels of silver, and one and one-half homers of barley. ³ And I said to her, "You shall stay with me many days; you shall not play the harlot, nor shall you have a man—so, too, will I be toward you."

In Joel (2:28–29) he is the *Baptizer with the Holy Spirit and Fire*:

And it shall come to pass afterward that I will pour out My Spirit on all flesh; Your sons and your daughters shall prophesy, Your old men shall dream dreams, Your young men shall see visions. ²⁹ And also on My menservants and on My maidservants, I will pour out My Spirit in those days.

In Amos (8:9–10) he is the *Burden-Bearer*:

"And it shall come to pass in that day," says the LORD God, "That I will make the sun go down at noon, and I will darken the earth in broad daylight; ¹⁰ I will turn your feasts into mourning, and all your songs into lamentation; I will bring sackcloth on every waist, and baldness on every head; I will make it like mourning for an only son, and its end like a bitter day."

In Obadiah (1:21) he is *Mighty to Save*:

Those who have been saved shall go up to Mount Zion to rule Mount Esau; and the kingdom shall be the LORD's.

In the book of Jonah (3:3–5) he is the *Great Foreign Missionary*:

So Jonah set out and went to Nineveh, according to the word of the LORD. Now Nineveh was an exceedingly large city, a three days' walk across. ⁴ Jonah began to go into the city, going a day's walk. And he cried out, "Forty days more, and Nineveh shall be overthrown!" ⁵ And the people of Nineveh believed God; they proclaimed a fast, and everyone, great and small, put on sackcloth.

In the book of Micah (5:2–5a) he is the *Messenger of Beautiful Feet*:

But you, O Bethlehem of Ephrathah, who are one of the little clans of Judah, from you shall come forth for me one who is to rule in Israel, whose origin is from of old, from ancient days. ³ Therefore he shall give them up until the time when she who is in labor has brought forth; then the rest of his kindred shall return to the people of Israel. ⁴ And he shall stand and feed his flock in the strength of the LORD, in the majesty of the name of the LORD his God. And they shall live secure, for now he shall be great to the ends of the earth; ⁵ and he shall be the one of peace.

In the book of Nahum (1:15) he is the *Avenger of God's Elect*:

Behold, on the mountains the feet of him who brings good tidings, who proclaims peace! O Judah, keep your appointed feasts, perform your vows. For the wicked one shall no more pass through you; he is utterly cut off.

In the book of Habakkuk (3:18–19), he is God's *Evangelist*:

Yet I will rejoice in the LORD, I will joy in the God of my salvation. ¹⁹ The LORD God is my strength; He will make my feet like deer's feet, and He will make me walk on my high hills.

In the book of Zephaniah (3:9) he is *Savior*:

For then I will restore to the peoples a pure language, that they all may call on the name of the LORD, to serve Him with one accord.

In the book of Haggai (2:6–9) he is the *Restorer of God's Lost Heritage*:

For thus says the LORD of hosts: "Once more (it is a little while) I will shake heaven and earth, the sea and dry land; ⁷ and I will shake all nations, and they shall come to the Desire of All Nations, and I will fill this temple with glory," says the LORD of hosts. ⁸ "The silver is Mine, and the gold is Mine," says the LORD of hosts. ⁹ "The glory of this latter temple shall be greater than the former," says the LORD of hosts. "And in this place, I will give peace," says the LORD of hosts."

In the book of Zechariah (14:8–9) he is the *Fountain Opened in the House of David for Sin and Uncleanness*:

"And in that day it shall be that living waters shall flow from Jerusalem, half of them toward the eastern sea and half of them toward the western sea; in both summer and winter it shall occur. ⁹ And the LORD shall be King over all the earth. In that day it shall be "The LORD is one," and His name one.

In the book of Malachi (4:2) he is *the Sun of Righteousness, Rising with Healing in His Wings*:

But to you who fear My name the Sun of Righteousness shall arise with healing in His wings; and you shall go out and grow fat like stall-fed calves.

In the book of Matthew (1:22–23) he is *Messiah*:

So all this was done that it might be fulfilled which was spoken by the Lord through the prophet, saying: [23] "Behold, the virgin shall be with child, and bear a Son, and they shall call His name Immanuel,: which is translated, "God with us."

In the book of Mark (1:27–28) he is the *Wonder-Worker*:

Then they were all amazed, so that they questioned among themselves, saying, "What is this? What new doctrine is this? For with authority, He commands even the unclean spirits, and they obey Him." [28] And immediately His fame spread throughout all the region around Galilee.

In the book of Luke (3:38) he is the *Son of Man*:

the son of Enosh, the son of Seth, the son of Adam, the son of God

In the book of John (3:16) he is the *Son of God*:

For God so loved the world that He gave His only begotten Son, that whoever believes in Him should not perish but have everlasting life.

In the book of Acts (2:31b–33) he is the *Holy Spirit*:

His soul was not left in Hades, nor did His flesh see corruption. [32] This Jesus God has raised up, of which we are all witnesses. [33] Therefore being exalted to the right hand of God, and having received from the Father the promise of the Holy Spirit, He poured out this which you now see and hear.

In the book of Romans (1:17) he is the *Justifier*:

For in it the righteousness of God is revealed from faith to faith; as it is written, "The just shall live by faith."

In First (1:30–31) and Second Corinthians he is the *Sanctifier*:

But of Him you are in Christ Jesus, who became for us wisdom from God—and righteousness and sanctification and redemption—[31]that, as it is written, "He who glories, let him glory in the Lord."

In the book of Galatians (3:13) he is the *Redeemer from the Curse of the Law*:

> Christ has redeemed us from the curse of the law, having become a curse for us (for it is written, "Cursed is everyone who hangs on a tree").

In the book of Ephesians (3:8–9) he is the *Christ of Unsearchable Riches*:

> To me, who am less than the least of all the saints, this grace was given, that I should preach among the Gentiles the unsearchable riches of Christ, ⁹ and to make all see what is the fellowship of the mystery, which from the beginning of the ages has been hidden in God who created all things through Jesus Christ.

In the book of Philippians (4:19) he is the *God Who Supplies All Our Needs*:

> And my God shall supply all your need according to His riches in glory by Christ Jesus.

In the book of Colossians (2:9–10), he is the *Fullness of the Godhead Bodily*:

> For in Him dwells all the fullness of the Godhead bodily; ¹⁰ and you are complete in Him, who is the head of all principality and power.

In First (3:13) and Second Thessalonians he is the *Soon-Coming King*:

> May he strengthen your hearts so that you will be blameless and holy in the presence of our God and Father when our Lord Jesus comes with all his holy ones.

In First (2:3–6) and Second Timothy he is the *Mediator between God and Man*:

> For this is good and acceptable in the sight of God our Savior, ⁴ who desires all men to be saved and to come to the knowledge of the truth. ⁵ For there is one God and one Mediator between God and men, the Man Christ Jesus, ⁶ who gave Himself a ransom for all, to be testified in due time.

In the book of Titus (2:11–14) he is the *Faithful Pastor*:

For the grace of God that brings salvation has appeared to all men, [12] teaching us that, denying ungodliness and worldly lusts, we should live soberly, righteously, and godly in the present age, [13] looking for the blessed hope and glorious appearing of our great God and Savior Jesus Christ, [14] who gave Himself for us, that He might redeem us from every lawless deed and purify for Himself His own special people, zealous for good works.

In the book of Philemon (7, 15–16) He is the *Friend Who Sticks Closer Than a Brother*:

For we have great joy and consolation in your love, because the hearts of the saints have been refreshed by you, brother. . . . [15] That you might receive him forever, [9] no longer as a slave but more than a slave—a beloved brother, especially to me but how much more to you, both in the flesh and in the Lord.

In the book of Hebrews (13:20–21) he is the *Blood of the Everlasting Covenant*:

Now may the God of peace who brought up our Lord Jesus from the dead, that great Shepherd of the sheep, through the blood of the everlasting covenant, [21] make you complete in every good work to do His will, working in you what is well pleasing in His sight, through Jesus Christ, to whom be glory forever and ever. Amen.

In the book of James (5:14–15) he is the *Great Physician*:

Is anyone among you sick? Let him call for the elders of the church, and let them pray over him, anointing him with oil in the name of the Lord. [15] And the prayer of faith will save the sick, and the Lord will raise him up. And if he has committed sins, he will be forgiven.

In First (5:4) and Second Peter he is the *Chief Shepherd*:

Aand when the Chief Shepherd appears, you will receive the crown of glory that does not fade away.

In First (4:7–11), Second, and Third John he is *Love*:

Beloved, let us love one another, for love is of God; and everyone who loves is born of God and knows God. [8] He who does not love does not know God, for God is love. [9] In this the love of God was manifested toward us, that God has sent His only begotten Son into the world, that we might live through Him. [10] In this is love, not that we loved God, but that He loved us and sent His Son to be the propitiation for our sins. [11] Beloved, if God so loved us, we also ought to love one another.

In the book of Jude (14) he is the *Lord Coming with Ten Thousands of His Saints*:

Now Enoch, the seventh from Adam, prophesied about these men also, saying, "Behold, the Lord comes with ten thousands of His saints."

In Revelation (19:13–16) he is the *King of Kings and Lord of Lords*:

He was clothed with a robe dipped in blood, and His name is called The Word of God. [14] And the armies in heaven, clothed in fine linen, white and clean, followed Him on white horses. [15] Now out of His mouth goes a sharp sword, that with it He should strike the nations. And He Himself will rule them with a rod of iron. He Himself treads the winepress of the fierceness and wrath of Almighty God. [16] And He has on His robe and on His thigh a name written:

KING OF KINGS AND
LORD OF LORDS.

Assertion after assertion that Jesus is the Thesis expressed throughout the entirety of Scripture. What are the ramifications of such emphatic claims? How might these profound truths impact humanity? What exactly do they mean for individuals? For nations? For people groups? For those answers, we will now turn to another preacher and another legendary sermon.

5

That's My King!

He's the greatest phenomenon that ever crossed the horizon of this
world. He's God's Son. He's a sinner's Savior. He's the centerpiece of
civilization. He stands in the solitude of Himself. He's august. He's unique.
He's unparalleled. He's unprecedented. He's the loftiest idea in literature.
He's the highest personality in philosophy. He's the supreme problem in
higher criticism. He's the fundamental doctrine of true theology. He's
the cardinal necessity of spiritual religion. He's the miracle of the age.
He's the superlative of everything good that you choose to call Him. He's
the only one qualified to be an all-sufficient Savior.

—S. M. LOCKRIDGE, "THAT'S MY KING"[1]

Reverend Shadrach Meshach

Through the preaching of his legendary "Fourth Man" sermon, mostly in
tent crusades across the United States, Oral Roberts repeatedly affirmed
Jesus's place as the Thesis of the biblical record and the focal point of the
Christian faith. Lives were changed, transformed, and healed, not only by
the content of the sermon but by the Fourth Man himself, the Lord Jesus
Christ. During the same period, another clarion voice touting the centrality of Jesus was legendary preacher S. M. Lockridge. Lockridge was senior

1. The reader is encouraged to listen to the entirety of Lockridge's sermon to give a
broader context to the material in this chapter. While many shorter versions exist, it is
highly encouraged that the longer version (about an hour) is accessed. In the bibliogra-
phy, see Lockridge, "That's My King," for the URL.

pastor at Calvary Baptist Church in San Diego, California, from 1953 to 1993. Amusingly, S. M. actually stands for Shadrach Meshach. So, the Rev. Shadrach Meshach Lockridge was used by God to preach one of the most famous sermons ever preached on American soil, entitled "That's My King." While thousands upon thousands heard it from Lockridge himself throughout the years, countless millions have listened on the internet. It is a vibrant, melodic, and energetic espousal of the true nature of Jesus that never gets old. So powerful and so profound that it warrants a deeper dive. If the reader has not already done so, he or she is strongly encouraged to take an hour, find it on the internet, buckle their seat belt, and prepare to be regaled with some of the best preaching ever heard.

Amen!

While Lockridge's sermon is primarily known for the repeated fiery, impassioned proclamations at the end of the sermon that attest to the greatness and grandness of King Jesus, they are made as a result of a systematic presentation of Jesus's own prayer in Matt 6:5–13. And while in his sermon he quotes the entirety of what is known as the Lord's Prayer, his focus is upon one word at the end of verse thirteen: "Amen." He asserts that in Luke 18:1, Jesus emphatically commands those who follow him to pray, "Then He spoke a parable to them, that men always ought to pray and not lose heart" (NKJV). "Always" and "ought" are commands that must be heeded. Most importantly however, Lockridge emphasizes the name in which the disciple prays. Certainly not in his own name.

For that would be to pray in the name of a mere mortal. One who would die and be forgotten. There was no power in praying like that. No, the follower of Jesus was to pray in Jesus's name.[2] That is where the power came from. And, while Jesus doesn't specifically command his disciples to pray in his name in Matt 6, he does say amen at the end of his prayer. Lockridge makes the powerful point that the amen was more than just an end to the prayer, but it had everything to do with the one in whose name the amen was proclaimed. The amen was so much more than an ending. It was in fact the beginning.[3] Once the amen was pronounced, the words to

2. While Jesus does not directly specify to use his name in Matt 6, the use of his name and its inherent power are emphasized in the following texts: John 14:13–14, 15:16, 16:23–24, 20:31; 1 Cor 1:2; Phil 2:9–11; Col 3:17.

3. The information in the next few paragraphs was not directly referred to by

the prayer were launched into effect. The content of the prayer was now out there in the atmosphere, empowered to do its work. The amen, especially spoken in the name of the Lord Jesus Christ, is literally a spiritual explosion. An explosion that warrants more attention.

Where Did It Come From?

Amen is ancient, appearing first in the Old Testament in the book of Numbers (5:22) and ultimately being used hundreds of times in both Testaments. It is what is known as a transliteration. That means that it is taken into other languages untranslated, as it is. It is amen in Hebrew, Greek, English and any other language in which it appears. Amen is amen. Some of the more prevalent places it is seen in the Bible are:

- It is the last word in the last verse of the Bible (Rev 22:21).
- It is the last word of the first three books of Psalms (41:13, 72:19, 89:52).
- It is the word spoken in the Old Testament by the community after a prophecy or proclamation was made (Neh 5:13, 8:6).
- It is the word used by Paul as an ending to many of his books. He also used amen seven times in the book of Romans (1:25, 9:5, 11:36, 15:33, 16:20, 24, 27).
- It is the word used by Jesus at the end of his teaching on prayer (Matt 6:13).
- Ultimately, Jesus would use it over fifty times, not only at the end of a statement but at the beginning, to introduce powerful truths (Matt 5:18).

Authoritative and Prophetic

While all of the instances outlined above certainly make amen a unique word, the prophet Isaiah takes it to another level of importance. He asserts that the amen is both authoritative and prophetic, in a messianic sense. In Isa 22:23, he states that the Messiah would be nailed in a "sure," "firm,"

Lockridge in his sermon but certainly emphasizes his point and provides a foundation for his legendary climax, which begins in the section entitled "The Seven-Way King".

or essentially an "amen" place. And in that place, he (the Messiah, Jesus) would be in a place of honor.[4] The one who would be nailed to the cross would be the final word and ultimately honored forever. Amen and amen!

> I will drive him like a peg into a firm place; he will become a seat of honor for the house of his father. [24] All the glory of his family will hang on him: its offspring and offshoots. (Isa 22:23–24)

In the deepest and most holistic sense, the amen is an affirmation and a blessing of the finished work of God.

Paul and the Amen

The apostle Paul affirmed repeatedly the power of the amen in many of his books, but especially in 2 Cor 1:20:

> For no matter how many promises God has made, they are "Yes" in Christ. And so through him the "Amen" is spoken by us to the glory of God.

In this text he cuts to the meat of the understanding of the amen. Jesus is in fact the amen. The final Word on all that is the focus of the kingdom community. For Paul, the amen was an assertion pointing towards the focal point of his gospel . . . Jesus, Jesus, Jesus.

Jesus and the Amen

In fact, Jesus himself gets the final word on the amen in the book of the Revelation as he refers to himself as "the Amen, the faithful and true witness, the Ruler of God's creation" (Rev. 3:14). John describes the reverberating effects brought on by beholding the amen as the hosts of heaven and earth behold him in his glory:

> Then I heard every creature in heaven and on earth and under the earth and on the sea, and all that is in them, saying: "To him who sits on the throne and to the Lamb be praise and honor and glory and power, for ever and ever!" [14] The four living creatures said, "Amen," and the elders fell down and worshiped. (Rev. 5:13–14)

4. 119 Ministries, "Hebrew Root of Amen."

The Seven-Way King

The authority and power of the amen is undisputed. An authority and power from which Lockridge launches a series of verbal lightning strikes pertaining to the manifold authority of the amen himself—King Jesus. A King whom Lockridge labels as the "Seven-Way King."

His first claim is that Jesus is the King of the Jews. This establishes Jesus as an ethnic king. Jesus affirms this himself in Mark 15:2:

> Then Pilate asked Him, "Are You the King of the Jews?"
> He answered and said to him, "It is as you say."

Lockridge's second claim is that Jesus is the King of Israel. This makes him a national king, affirmed in the Old Testament in Num 24:17:

> I see Him, but not now;
> I behold Him, but not near;
> A Star shall come out of Jacob;
> A Scepter shall rise out of Israel,
> And batter the brow of Moab,
> And destroy all the sons of tumult.

The prophet Micah declares in Micah 5:2:

> But you, Bethlehem Ephrathah,
> Though you are little among the thousands of Judah,
> Yet out of you shall come forth to Me
> The One to be Ruler in Israel,
> Whose goings forth are from of old,
> From everlasting.

In Matt 2:5–6 he is recognized by the wise men:

> In Bethlehem of Judea, for thus it is written by the prophet:
> ⁶ "But you, Bethlehem, in the land of Judah,
> Are not the least among the rulers of Judah;
> For out of you shall come a Ruler
> Who will shepherd My people Israel."

Nathanael, a newly recruited disciple who had only just met him affirmed Jesus as King in the Gospel of John (1:49):

> Nathanael answered and said to Him, "Rabbi, You are the Son of God! You are the King of Israel!"

Even those who mocked him unknowingly affirmed his royalty as the King of Israel in Mark 15:31–32:

> Likewise the chief priests also, mocking among themselves with the scribes, said, "He saved others; Himself He cannot save. [32] Let the Christ, the King of Israel, descend now from the cross, that we may see and believe."

Lockridge's third claim is that Jesus is the King of righteousness. He notes that this sets him apart as the one and only monarch who would rule and reign righteously, in and of himself. No one else made him righteous. The prophet Isaiah spoke of his rule in Isa 32:1:

> Behold, a king will reign in righteousness.

The writer of Hebrews explains that Jesus would be Priest and King in Hebrews 7:1–3:

> For this Melchizedek, king of Salem, priest of the Most High God, who met Abraham returning from the slaughter of the kings and blessed him, [2] to whom also Abraham gave a tenth part of all, first being translated "king of righteousness," and then also king of Salem, meaning "king of peace," [3] without father, without mother, without genealogy, having neither beginning of days nor end of life, but made like the Son of God, remains a priest continually.

Fourth, Lockridge hails Jesus as the King of the ages. Affirmed by John in the book of Revelation (11:15):

> Then the seventh angel sounded: And there were loud voices in heaven, saying, "The kingdoms of this world have become the kingdoms of our Lord and of His Christ, and He shall reign forever and ever!"

Fifth, Lockridge declares that Jesus is the King of heaven. This was first announced to Mary by the angel in Luke 1:31–33:

> And behold, you will conceive in your womb and bring forth a Son and shall call His name Jesus. [32] He will be great and will be called the Son of the Highest; and the Lord God will give Him the throne of His father David. [33] And He will reign over the house of Jacob forever, and of His kingdom there will be no end.

Sixth, Lockridge declares that Jesus is the King of glory. Psalm 24:7–10 sings:

Lift up your heads, O you gates!
And be lifted up, you everlasting doors!
And the King of glory shall come in.
⁸ Who is this King of glory?
The LORD strong and mighty,
The LORD mighty in battle.
⁹ Lift up your heads, O you gates!
Lift up, you everlasting doors!
And the King of glory shall come in.
¹⁰ Who is this King of glory?
The LORD of hosts,
He is the King of glory.

The apostle Paul adds in 1 Cor 2:7–8:

> But we speak the wisdom of God in a mystery, the hidden wisdom which God ordained before the ages for our glory, ⁸ which none of the rulers of this age knew; for had they known, they would not have crucified the Lord of glory.

Seventh, Lockridge's case crescendos in the affirmation that Jesus is the King of kings and the Lord of lords. He is the superlative Deity. He is the matchless One. In Deut 10:17 Moses declares that:

> The LORD your God is God of gods and Lord of lords, the great God, mighty and awesome, who shows no partiality nor takes a bribe.

The psalmist agrees in Ps 136:3:

> Oh, give thanks to the Lord of lords!
> For His mercy endures forever.

The apostle Paul describes his matchless power and position in 1 Tim 6:15b–16:

> He who is the blessed and only Potentate, the King of kings and Lord of lords, ¹⁶ who alone has immortality, dwelling in unapproachable light, whom no man has seen or can see, to whom be honor and everlasting power. Amen.

John regales him repeatedly with the highest praise in Revelation:

> To Him who loved us and washed us from our sins in His own blood, ⁶ and has made us kings and priests to His God and Father to Him be glory and dominion forever and ever. Amen. ⁷ Behold,

He is coming with clouds, and every eye will see Him, even they
who pierced Him. And all the tribes of the earth will mourn because of Him. Even so, Amen. (Rev 1:5b–7)

For He is Lord of lords and King of kings; and those who are with
Him are called, chosen, and faithful. (Rev 17:14b)

And He has on His robe and on His thigh a name written:
KING OF KINGS AND
LORD OF LORDS. (Rev 19:16)

Amen and a thousand more amens!

A Thousand More?

Listening to these classic sermons over the last few years has stirred something in me (Jeff). Stirred me to the point that I believe Jesus, the amen
himself, deserves much more than one word at the end of a prayer signal-
ing listeners to go back to life and business as usual. Something needed
to change. The ordinary rhythm needed to be broken. But how? All of us
know that in order to change something that has become rote and lifeless, something new would need to be interjected. What would that be? I
couldn't make up my own word; that could be heretical, and heresies are
frowned upon.

I began to find myself wanting to say something like "Amen and a lot
more amens." That didn't flow very well. There were a couple more phrases
I tried that didn't work either. They were clumsy and cumbersome at best.
Then, almost as if it were dropped from heaven, to my mind, then off of
my lips, I exclaimed after a passionate prayer, "Amen and a thousand more
amens!" It felt really good. And while I know that the Amen is in and of
itself infinitely more than a thousand, a thousand is still quite a few and
makes an emphatic statement. So, I started saying "Amen and a thousand
more amens" in my personal devotions. I noticed that it felt different but
good. I liked how it caused me to linger a bit and to think about the amen
and what I had said before it. And, if Jesus, the amen, is to be remembered
authoritatively when it is said, a thousand more for emphasis is a good
thing. A very good thing. A thousand more good things.

Ultimately, I began to say "Amen and a thousand more amens" after preaching sermons on Sundays, after class lectures and speaking

engagements. At first people were taken aback, but it began to catch on. People in my circles have now begun to expect it and will even finish the sentence with me. It has spurred quite a few conversations regarding the amen, which ultimately lead back to Jesus and his supreme authority. That is always a good thing; for he is the only reason that our prayers have any power and lingering effect anyway. He is the Thesis and center of kingdom strategy. So, a hearty amen and a thousand more to him as the Fourth Man, the Seven-Way King, and ultimately as our victorious Serpent Crusher. It is that third title to which we will now turn our attention.

6

Serpent Crusher

And I will put enmity between you and the woman, and between your offspring and hers; he will *crush* your head, and you will strike his heel.

—GEN 3:15 NIV (EMPHASIS ADDED)

If only for this life we have hope in Christ, we are of all people most to be pitied. [20] But Christ has indeed been raised from the dead, the firstfruits of those who have fallen asleep. [21] For since death came through a man, the resurrection of the dead comes also through a man. [22] For as in Adam all die, so in Christ all will be made alive. [23] But each in turn: Christ, the firstfruits; then, when he comes, those who belong to him. [24] Then the end will come, when he hands over the kingdom to God the Father after he has destroyed [crushed] all dominion, authority and power. [25] For he must reign until he has put all his enemies *under his feet*.

—1 COR 15:19–25 NIV (EMPHASIS ADDED)

Coup de Grâce

IT IS CERTAINLY COMPELLING that Jesus was the Fourth Man in Daniel and the focal point of every book in the Bible. His seven-way kingship is also impressive, to say the least. He is undoubtedly the cohesive factor that binds together all sixty-six books of the canon. However, this is not enough. Yes, I said it. It's not enough. Jesus in every book and Jesus as a powerful and influential King are simply not enough. They are not enough because the Bible's ultimate coup de grâce is that Jesus Christ is the Serpent Crusher. If he doesn't crush the serpent, he is the one who gets crushed. And the ultimate crushing blow to any and all of us is death. Death is the blow that crushes the life out of us and ultimately wins . . . unless.

Unless there is something after death. Something more than death. Something that crushes death. Someone or something that goes beyond death and reverses the crushing curse that it brings upon humanity. This is the story about which we have spoken in earlier chapters as we examined mythopoeia, the true myth (ch. 1) and the eucatastrophic hope (ch. 2) that exists in us all. A story that is written into many cultures due to the inherent hope that is present in all men (ch. 1)—a hope that there is someone or something beyond the crush of death—beyond the end of this life.

The Proto-Evangelium

To understand why this is the case, we must go back to the beginning. In the beginning, God created man, Adam, then placed him on the earth to establish dominion on his behalf (Gen 1:26–28). Eve would be God's crowning gift to him. A suitable partner with whom he could live, love, and serve the Creator (Gen 2:18–25). Together the three of them, Adam, Eve, and their Creator would build his kingdom on earth. A kingdom that would be an open expression of the Creator's love and desire to be loved in return. This rhythm of life went well for a period of time. For exactly how long, we don't know; but we do know that it was very good (Gen 1:31).

Together they would work and serve and build and love; until, one day, or for a period of days, the serpent walked into the garden, and seduced Eve.[1] That shiny, conniving, seductive wretch assaulted her. He called into question the Creator's motives and plan (Gen 3:1–4). He even did so while the inattentive Adam sat with her. The narrative explains that Eve took some of the forbidden fruit and gave it to Adam, "for he was with her" (Gen 3:1–7). He allowed for her to be lied to and the Creator to be disparaged. This set of tyrannical circumstances brought upon them, and all of their descendants, an eternal curse. A curse that has been deemed as the "fall." Yes, a crushing, reverberating death-nail to their relationship with the

---

1. It is our personal opinion that the serpent walked for a period of time, until the curse sentenced him to crawl on his belly (Gen 3:15).

Creator. His plans for an earthly kingdom were doomed. Their dominion was crushed. Hope was lost eternally. Or was it?

Absolutely not. But it would not, could not be reclaimed without a great price being paid. The Godhead had a plan. A plan that would be played out over the ensuing generations. A plan that is chronicled in the Bible and ultimately comes to fruition in the person of Jesus Christ. Yes, Jesus Christ was in fact the Thesis in the garden. A prophetic hope on the darkest of all days. Theologians call it the *proto-evangelium*, a term that means "first gospel." In the midst of the cataclysmic first fall, there was also a literal first seed of evangelistic hope. A seed that would travel miraculously through the generations.

The perfect seed of heaven would somehow be carried by specific, chosen, imperfect individuals; then, at the perfect time (Gal 4:4–7), the seed would be vivified divinely by God's Spirit. Brought to life and placed into a woman, it would grow as the God-Man, Jesus. He would be the One who would crush the head of the serpent. He would become the killer of death, dying sacrificially on behalf of fallen mankind (Rev 13:8).[2] The God-Man, Jesus, would ultimately crush the one who had introduced disobedience, death, and all of their heinous by-products into the garden. Genesis 3:14–15 recounts the events of that dark, prophetic, serpent-crushing day. The great English preacher Charles Simeon aptly called these verses "the sum and summary of the whole Bible":[3]

> So the Lord God said to the serpent, "Because you have done this,
> "Cursed are you above all livestock and all wild animals! You will
> crawl on your belly and you will eat dust all the days of your life.
> [15] And I will put enmity between you and the woman, and between
> your offspring (seed) and hers; he will crush your head, and you
> will strike his heel." (Gen 3:14–15 NIV)

From this proclamation forward, we are privy in the biblical narrative to the historic battle between the seeds. The seed of the serpent versus the kingdom-seed of the woman. An eerie proclamation it was. Warfare and hatred between the seeds of the woman and the serpent. The serpent, not allowed to speak again, is cursed[4] by the Creator's own voice. Con-

2. In ch. 8, "For Our Sake," we explain this in greater detail.

3. Simeon, "Discourse 7."

4. Waltke, *Genesis*, 93. Waltke notes that this curse means the serpent, who is either Satan himself, or an animal in whom Satan has taken residence, is not allowed to speak again. His/their seed is also "consigned to impotence" and will not have the "productivity

demned to slither and grovel in the dirt (Gen 3:14). The man and woman, sentenced to live lives filled with turmoil, struggle, and pain (Gen 3:16-19). Pain experienced in banishment from their once paradisiacal home (Gen 3:23-24). Primal innocence, freedom, and transparency (Gen 2:25) were now eternally tainted as they skulked in shameful defeat (Gen 3:8-10). In a foreshadowing of what was to come, however (Rev 13:8), the Creator would himself sacrifice innocent blood in order to cover them (Gen 3:21). The hope of the kingdom-seed would be there, always hidden in the protective cleft of relationship with the Creator.

Covering, cursing, falling, and banishment; the garden tragedy was of epic proportions and bore epic consequences. Consequences that reverberate into every life and every family that has come forth on this planet since that dark day. All of humanity is birthed into the bloody battlefield of those consequences—a battlefield called earth. And although the Bible provides a plethora of examples as to the crushing effects of the battle over a period of many thousands of years, we will focus only on several pivotal instances in the battle between the seeds.

Assault on the First Family

For the first family, life outside of the garden was destined towards hardship, struggle, and death. The battle between the seeds would visit them in treacherous fashion. Eve would give a hint as to how this treachery would come to fruition at the announcement of the birth of her firstborn son, "With the help of the Lord, I have brought forth a man" (Gen 4:1b). While it may seem that she gives at least some credit to God for his part in the process, she is essentially saying that Cain's birth was something that she had done. This announcement is in stark contradistinction to other God-ordered births in Scripture, such as Hannah giving birth to Samuel (1 Sam 1:21—2:10), where she gives full credit to God and to him alone. Mary, the mother of Jesus, also gives glory to God for what he would do (Luke 1:46-55).

The two women seem to have had a totally different perspective than Eve. Waltke states that as a result of her taking credit for Cain's birth, "The reader is signaled to expect problems in the life and line of Cain."[5]

---

of God upon it. It cannot overcome final death to live forever." On the other hand, the seed of the woman will in fact possess the productivity of God upon it.

5. Waltke, *Genesis*, 96.

Ultimately, in addition to the firstborn Cain, Adam and Eve would have a second son, Abel (Gen 4:2). While the Genesis narrative doesn't give many specifics as to why it is so, other than Eve's apparent hubris tainting Cain's birth, Abel was much different than Cain. The writer of Hebrews states in affirmation of his character, that he was "righteous" (11:4 NIV). Obviously, the narrative is recounting that the seeds were at odds from the beginning and would seek habitation in the first family.

After their parents, these two sons would be the first on the planet to decide whether they would be a seedbed for the seed of the serpent or the seed of the kingdom. Would they perpetuate the Creator's plan or the serpent's? The choice came presented to the sons as a result of the status of their hearts regarding the bringing of offerings to God. Abel, a shepherd, brought the first and best of his flock. Cain, a man of the fields, brought only some of his harvest (Gen 4:2b–5). God accepted Abel's offering but rejected Cain's. This angered Cain so deeply that he lured Abel to his field, then like a ravenous lion in his lair, murdered his younger brother there (Gen 4:8–9).

The serpent's seed, planted in the field of Cain's heart, yielded a crop that would manifest as the serpent's lineage of death throughout the ages. The apostle John gives further insight into Cain and his diabolical choice as he states that Cain "belonged to the evil one and murdered his brother" (1 John 3:12 NIV). The "belonging" to which John refers is believed by some scholars to infer that Cain was literally the seed of the serpent. He belonged to him, because he was of his seed. Cain had given himself over so totally to the serpent that he was now about the death and destruction that were indicative of the serpent.[6]

He had ignored God's voice. A voice that had beckoned him to turn from the seeds of sin and death that were "crouching" at the door of his heart (Gen 4:6–7 NIV). The "enmity" prophesied in Gen 3:15 had become a deadly reality. The first family had been tainted once again. The sin of the parents visited upon their children. Cain's sinful, serpent-induced choice had yielded a crop of death. The seed of the serpent had been implanted into his mind, then received into his heart. A deadly entity was now ruling Cain's life and ultimately his line. The seed of the serpent versus the

---

6. Currid, "Introduction to Biblical Theology," 21. Currid, in his seventh lecture of a series entitled "Introduction to Biblical Theology," emphasizes this point thoroughly. He feels that Cain was of the evil one and would eventually disobey, renounce and endeavor to thwart God's plans whenever and wherever he could. His progeny would perpetuate and take his sinful and disobedient actions throughout the ages.

kingdom-seed of the woman. The serpent had attempted to eradicate the seed by killing Abel, its human seedbed. Seemingly, this round in the cosmic fight for the souls of all humanity had certainly gone to the serpent.

However, the omniscient Creator always has a plan and is ultimately and eternally one step ahead of the serpent. The writer of Hebrews affirms this as he asserts that the faith of Abel actually cried out to heaven from the earth, through his innocent blood (Heb 11:4, 12:24). The seed was in fact not dead. It was very much alive and being incubated by faith and readied for the next carrier. Then, in Gen 4, the next carrier in the line of the kingdom-seed of the woman is born:

> Adam made love to his wife again, and she gave birth to a son and named him Seth, saying, "God has granted me another child in place of Abel, since Cain killed him." [26] Seth also had a son, and he named him Enosh.
> At that time people began to call on the name of the LORD.
> (Gen 4:25–26)

Three important discoveries are to be gleaned from this text. First, the ancient reader would have undoubtedly known that the name Seth meant "granted," or "to set, or place."[7] Through the mouth of Eve, the narrator was letting the reader know that God had granted someone to take Abel's place in the lineage of the kingdom-seed of the woman. There was to be no question that the seed lived in Seth. Second, in the birth of this son, Eve has given God full credit for replacing Abel. After the debacle with Cain, she now knew that she was merely the vessel, he the sole Progenitor. Third, with hope alive and the seed perpetuated, people "began to call on the name of the LORD."[8] In replacing Abel with Seth, God was undoubtedly affirming that the seed would always survive. It would survive in, and be perpetuated by, faith. The faith of the chosen ones who believed in him, called upon him, and obeyed his eternal word. A prophetic word that would miraculously bring into existence a second Adam, who would ultimately, once and for all, crush the head of the serpent.[9] The biblical narrative is an ever-present reminder of the generations who were engaged in the crushing battle between the seeds.

---

7. Waltke, *Genesis*, 101.

8. Waltke, *Genesis*, 101.

9. Waltke, *Genesis* 103–5.

The Battle Rages and the Seed Is Saved

The text of Gen 5 provides a specific lineage for the kingdom-seed of the woman, carried by Seth and his descendants through seven generations over 777 years.[10] And while not many details are given as to exactly how it came about, culture became so decadent during that time period that even the progeny of the kingdom-seed had to be admonished (Gen 6:1–4). God therefore made a plan for an earthly, cataclysmic reset. In Gen 6, the narrator sets the stage:

> The LORD saw how great the wickedness of the human race had become on the earth, and that every inclination of the thoughts of the human heart was only evil all the time. [6] The LORD regretted that he had made human beings on the earth, and his heart was deeply troubled. [7] So the LORD said, "I will wipe from the face of the earth the human race I have created—and with them the animals, the birds and the creatures that move along the ground—for I regret that I have made them." [8] But Noah found favor in the eyes of the Lord. [9] This is the account of Noah and his family. Noah was a righteous man, blameless among the people of his time, and he walked faithfully with God. (Gen 6:5–9 NIV)[11]

So rampant was evil only a few short generations after Seth's birth that "every inclination of the thoughts of the human heart was only evil all the time" (Gen 6:5b). "Every" and "all" the time? These are strong descriptors. Evil was most assuredly at the core of culture and ruled the day. The battle between the seeds raged on. In 777 years (a short span in the context of history), the entirety of culture was evil. Every aspect of human engagement had become debased. However, the text does not fail to point out that the eyes of God, in his grace,[12] were looking for someone to perpetuate

10. The number seven and its multiples are particularly important in the biblical narrative. The fact of the seventh generation and of it occurring after 777 years cannot go unnoticed. The narrator is indicating that something of great importance is about to happen.

11. The reader is encouraged to remember the discussion of the "true myth" in ch. 1, especially where it pointed towards epic cosmologies in other cultures, including epics such as *Gilgamesh* and some of the other less known ones noted by Richardson in *Eternity in Their Hearts*. It is here where the Judeo-Christian telling of this epic cosmology is to be seen as the most true and accurate—the one where the kingdom-seed of the woman would be perpetuated forward, ultimately to result in the birth of Jesus. See also Waltke, *Genesis*, 118, for more on this subject.

12. Currid, "Introduction to Biblical Theology," 25. This is the first time in Scripture

the seed. God found Noah. Noah, in his obedience, responded to God's gracious overture. He built an ark, then with his family sailed as God's kingdom-seed through the cataclysmic flood. A flood that destroyed all life on the earth, except for that which was with him on the ark (Gen 6—9:1). Eventually the ark would deliver the kingdom-seed safely to dry ground, perpetuated by a covenant blessing and accompanying command:

> Then God blessed Noah and his sons, saying to them, "Be fruitful and increase in number and fill the earth. ²The fear and dread of you will fall on all the beasts of the earth, and on all the birds in the sky, on every creature that moves along the ground, and on all the fish in the sea; they are given into your hands. ³Everything that lives and moves about will be food for you. Just as I gave you the green plants, I now give you everything. (Gen 9:1–3 NIV)

Undoubtedly, the command to "increase in number and fill the earth" was an allusion to the fact that the kingdom-seed, in accordance with the proto-evangelium of Gen 3:14–15, would continue forward and increase upon the battleground that was the earth. The seed would increase, being endowed with authority to exercise "fear and dread . . . on all the beasts of the earth . . . and on every creature that moves along the ground" (Gen 6:2 NIV). One cannot help but remember the prophetic pronouncement pertaining to the seed of the woman, which would ultimately crush the head of the serpent. A loud echo reverberates through Gen 6:2.

While the kingdom-seed of the woman was perpetuated by Noah, the serpent's seed survived the cataclysm as well. Through the ensuing ages, both would take root in the hearts of humans who would become fertile ground for them. The serpent-seed always seeking those who would question God and deify their own lust-filled appetites. The kingdom-seed of the woman seeking obedient hearts focused upon God's plan for redemption and establishing his kingdom dominion. The battle between the two, pointing always towards the final crushing of the serpent's head at some point in history.

Following Seth and Noah as carriers of the seed, Noah's son Shem is singled out. In Gen 9:26b, a prophetic utterance from the mouth of Noah himself affirms:[13]

---

where the term *favor* is used. It is synonymous with grace. Grace is therefore not to be seen solely as a concept introduced in the New Testament. God is a God of grace throughout the entirety of the Bible.

13. Waltke, *Genesis*, 151. This blessing is seen as Noah's affirmation that it would in

Praise be to the Lord, the God of Shem!

Through Shem, the seed, having survived the flood, is passed through the generations by Abraham (Gen 12:1–3; 14:18–20), Isaac (Gen 17:19), Jacob (Gen 35:9–15) and select others, ultimately to be fully born as the Serpent Crusher, Jesus. In each of these instances the providence of God is affirmed, a blessing given, and the carrier of the seed commended to go forward in faith on behalf of the God who had taken notice of them. The progression of the seed into the life of Jesus is chronicled in the Gospel narrative, specifically in Luke 3:21–38, and includes both famous and obscure individuals. While we will examine the Lukan lineage in an upcoming section, we have chosen here to highlight only a few of the serpent-crushing, seed-carrying individuals—ones chosen specifically by God over the millennia to point towards the ultimate Serpent Crusher himself.

Serpent-Crushing Highlights

Theologian James Hamilton of Harvard Divinity School states in his article "The Skull Crushing Seed of the Woman":

> Bad guys get broken heads in the Bible. In some texts it is specifically stated that the ones shattered are serpents. The serpent was told he would eat dust (Gen 3:14), and in several places the rebellious eat or lick dust. At points, a number of these images are used together, but the enmity between the seeds and some aspect of the curse are present in them all.[14]

In all due respect to Dr. Hamilton and a litany of other scholars who have written on this subject in compelling fashion, it doesn't take someone with a PhD to know that a serpent's head needs to be dealt with to finish the job entirely. It's in the head where the brain lives, thinking occurs, and strategies are planned. It is the head that needs to be smashed and pummeled into lifelessness. Whether that be through impaling, hanging, beheading, or crushing—everyone knows that. A few biblical examples of the serpent's

---

fact be Shem's line through which God would ultimately rule and reign on the earth. Waltke suggests that "this is the first indication that God elects the line of Shem to rule the earth (Gen. 1:26–28) and crush the Serpent (Gen. 3:15; 4:26). Sovereign grace always opens a blessed future, as when God chooses as Shem's successors, Abraham, not Nahor; Isaac, not Ishmael; Jacob, not Esau; Judah, not Joseph."

14. Hamilton, "Skull Crushing Seed," 34.

head being crushed in some form or fashion in the Old Testament are as follows:

1. A woman named Jael (heroine) drives a peg through Sisera's (serpent-seed) head (Judg 4, 5:26).

2. An unknown woman (heroine) throws a millstone from a wall onto Abimelech's (evil king, serpent-seed) head (Judg 9:53).

3. Haman (serpent-seed) is hanged by the neck on gallows he had prepared for Esther's (heroine) uncle (Esth 7).

4. Yahweh crushes the head "from the house of the wicked" (Hab 3:13 NIV).[15]

While there are many more examples that could bolster the case being made for God's continual reminding his people, and the serpent as well, that he had not forgotten his prophecy in Gen 3:15, there is one reminder that stands out in grander fashion than all the others. This has to do mostly with the reputation and size of the carrier of the serpent's seed and the short-lived anonymity of the one carrying the kingdom-seed of the woman.

A Giant Serpent

In 1 Sam 17 one of the most epic serpent-crushing tales in all of literature exists, that being the battle between David and Goliath.[16] The unknown shepherd, David, Son of Jesse (1 Sam 16:11) is identified by God to Samuel, the prophet/judge (1 Sam 16:12), and anointed king (1 Sam 16:13). He would be identified for his God-focused "heart" (1 Sam 16:7 NIV) and not necessarily his physical appearance. At his intimate anointing ceremony before his family and God, the narrative informs the reader that the Spirit, in fact, "came upon David in power" (1 Sam 16:13 NIV).

The fact that God had come "upon David in power" most assuredly harkens back to Abel, Seth, Noah, Abraham, Isaac, Jacob, and eventually

15. Hamilton, "Skull Crushing Seed," 36.

16. The reader is encouraged to read 1 Sam 16 and 17 in their entirety for a more holistic understanding of the magnitude of this battle, as well as some of the accompanying details and individuals involved. This unique interaction between the Philistine and Israelite armies is an epic battle in all military history. Moreover, it is a watershed moment in the perpetuation of the kingdom-seed of the woman, as one of its most famous carriers, David, delivers a crushing blow to one of the serpent-seeds most infamous, Goliath of Gath.

their progeny as well. God had noticed and singled out the young man David, just like he had done in the case of the other seed carriers. Although he was anonymous to others and not even revered in his own household, he had been singled out by God to carry the kingdom-seed. In fact, his name is listed in both lineages of the ultimate Serpent Crusher, Jesus (Matt 1:1, 6; Luke 3:31). King David would be used to carry the seed and perpetuate it to Jesus. Jesus would in fact be called the "Son of David" on several occasions (Matt 1:1, Mark 12:35–37, Luke 1:32). This sonship would rightfully place him on the throne of David as the eternal heir to the promise of God to David in 2 Sam 7:16: "Your house and your kingdom shall be made sure forever before me; your throne shall be established forever" (NIV). Jesus Christ would therefore be known as the Son of David[17] and would rightfully inherit his, David's, throne. The kingdom-seed of the woman, the eternal Serpent Crusher, would be an eternal King. As the anointed king of his nation and carrier of the serpent-crushing seed, God intended to use this young man in extraordinary fashion and thereby make an extraordinarily loud and large statement to all the world.[18]

The stage for this historic battle was the valley of Elah, which was only fifteen miles west of David's hometown of Bethlehem and twelve miles from Hebron, the young nation's first home base. It was essentially right down the street in military terms. For some undisclosed reason, the leaders had chosen the type of conflict that called for two champions to meet in front of their respective armies, then fight to the death, with the winner taking all the spoils. And by all the spoils, it was known that family, livestock, land, and everything else that a man owned would become property of the victor. Hope was nowhere to be found. This was due greatly to the fact that King Saul, the supposed champion of God's army, was hiding in his tent, while a Philistine giant named Goliath appeared daily, heaving vile curses and threats at them.

What seemed to be certain defeat hung over the battlefield like a thick fog. There was neither a plan nor a ray of hope (1 Sam 17:1–11). The serpent's seed had certainly slithered into the dominant position. Kingdom-seed was once again on the brink of extinction. However, with God and the perpetuation of his seed, hope is eternal; and, as has been seen in this

17. While Jesus Christ would in fact be the rightful heir to the throne of David, he was also David's Lord. David prophetically saw and stated this in Ps 110:1. The apostle Peter affirms this and expounds upon it in Acts 2:29–33.

18. We would once again recommend that you read the entirety of this narrative (1 Sam 16–17), and especially review 1 Sam 17:40–58 for a greater context.

age-old enmity-filled conflict, it often shines in unlikely places and through unassuming, faith-filled faces. On that day, in the valley of Elah, the face belonged to a ruddy teenager (1 Sam 16:12), who had been sent from Bethlehem by his father to take food to his brothers who were on the battle lines, hiding in intimidation (1 Sam 17:17–22). A faith-filled face that would beam brightly from the light of a fire-kindled heart. A fire that would not be doused by intimidating words or actions.

The intimidating words were ultimately hurled directly at David as he bravely volunteered to confront the giant, then calmly stepped onto the battlefield with his pouch, five smooth stones, sling, and staff (1 Sam 17:40):

> He said to David, "Am I a dog, that you come at me with sticks?" And the Philistine cursed David by his gods. 44 "Come here," he said, "and I'll give your flesh to the birds and the wild animals!" (1 Sam 17:43–44 NIV)

The seed of the serpent and the kingdom-seed of the woman face-to-face in a duel with ancient implements of war and eternal implications. Huge spears, slings, stones, javelins, and swords were at the ready. The carrier of the kingdom-seed responded with steely courage, tethered to the name and reputation of his God—the God whom he knew personally and who had uttered the proto-evangelium himself, thousands of years before:

> David said to the Philistine, "You come against me with sword and spear and javelin, but I come against you in the name of the Lord Almighty, the God of the armies of Israel, whom you have defied. 46 This day the LORD will deliver you into my hands, and I'll strike you down and cut off your head. This very day I will give the carcasses of the Philistine army to the birds and the wild animals, and the whole world will know that there is a God in Israel. 47 All those gathered here will know that it is not by sword or spear that the LORD saves; for the battle is the LORD's, and he will give all of you into our hands." (1 Sam 17:45–47 NIV)

Like a flash of lightning, and as he had certainly done thousands of times before while tending his father's sheep, David reached into his pouch, loaded a stone, then slung it from his sling towards the huge target lumbering towards him. The crush was quick and deep, followed by an earth-shaking thud. A cloud of dust rose as the onlookers stared in disbelief. The narrative recounts those epic moments:

David ran quickly toward the battle line to meet him. [49] Reaching into his bag and taking out a stone, he slung it and struck the Philistine on the forehead. The stone sank into his forehead, and he fell facedown on the ground. [50] So David triumphed over the Philistine with a sling and a stone; without a sword in his hand he struck down the Philistine and killed him. [51] David ran and stood over him. He took hold of the Philistine's sword and drew it from the sheath. After he killed him, he cut off his head with the sword. (1 Sam 17:48b–51)

In a few short seconds, the tide had turned. Hope now shone brightly through the settling dust of Elah's battlefield. The head of the giant seed of the serpent had been stealthily crushed, then decapitated for all the world to see. There was a new champion. One who, with a bloody trophy in his hands, would scream loudly that there was a God in his nation. A serpent crusher who would always deliver. David would harken back to that glorious day often in his psalms:

> Surely God will crush the heads of his enemies, the hairy crowns of those who go on in their sins. (Ps 68:21 NIV)

> But God is my King from long ago; he brings salvation on the earth. It was you who split open the sea by your power; you broke the heads of the monster in the waters. It was you who crushed the heads of Leviathan and gave it as food to the creatures of the desert. (Ps 74:12–14)

An Important Detail

Certainly, that day for David marked his life and has remained as one of the most epic battles ever to occur on this planet. Almost everyone knows about it, whether they are religious or not. The victory of the giant-slaying serpent crusher reverberates still. However, for all the details that are provided in the narrative in 1 Sam 16–17, there is one that initially perplexed me (Jeff). Perplexed me until I dove into it a bit more. That detail has to do with the eventual resting place of the head of Goliath. While it may sound barbaric, it is a detail that I feel warrants a search and has major implications. It was a focal point of the battle and mentioned more than once. It was most certainly a triumphal trophy. That being understood, where might David have displayed it? I believe that he most probably did display it, as that was a gruesome custom of the day. Evidenced by the fact that the same thing would happen (most probably in retribution for the Goliath killing) to King Saul and his sons after they were killed in battle:

> The next day, when the Philistines came to strip the dead, they found Saul and his three sons fallen on Mount Gilboa. [9] They cut off his head, stripped off his armor, and sent messengers throughout the land of the Philistines to carry the good news to the houses of their idols and to the people. [10] They put his armor in the temple of Astarte; and they fastened his body to the wall of Beth-shan. (1 Sam 31:8–10 NIV)

The narrative in this instance is specific as to the fact that the trophies were displayed and where they were displayed as well. Therefore, it is fair to assume that David might have done the same thing. In an effort to discover where the Goliath trophy might have been kept, one would first have to go where it was last seen. In the 1 Sam 17 narrative it was in fact last seen in verses 54 and 57:

> David took the *Philistine's head* and brought it to Jerusalem; he put the Philistine's weapons in his own tent. [55] As Saul watched David going out to meet the Philistine, he said to Abner, commander of the army, "Abner, whose son is that young man?" Abner replied, "As surely as you live, Your Majesty, I don't know." [56] The king said, "Find out whose son this young man is." [57] As soon as David returned from killing the Philistine, Abner took him and brought him before Saul, with David still holding the *Philistine's head*. (1 Sam 17:54–57 NIV; emphases added)

Jerusalem is where David is said to have taken the head, while initially keeping Goliath's weapons in his own tent (1 Sam 17:54). After these references to the trophies, there is one more reference regarding the sword, as it was eventually located in the city of Nob, behind the priest's ephod (1 Sam 21:9). The fact that it made its way into such a revered place indicates, once again, that these types of relics were commonly put on display or at least kept for use on special occasions. But, where might the head, a glorious reminder of one of the most important military victories in the history of God's people and, for that matter, salvation history, end up being located?

Dr. Taylor Marshall hypothesizes that such a famous relic was displayed in a famously infamous place:

> This would explain why the "place of the skull" is oddly named "Golgotha." The term is a corruption of Hebrew for "Goliath Gath":

Goliath Gath > GoliGath > GolGath > GolGatha So King David killed the enemy of Israel (Goliath of Gath) and then brought the giant's head to Jerusalem. Jews would not have permitted the Gentile giant's head to be buried in the city walls. It would have been buried outside the city walls. This matches with what we know about the location of Golgatha. It was outside the city walls. The slaying of Goliath by David was one of the most important events in "Israelite history." The location of the giant's head would have been known by all. Hence, "Golgatha" is likely the the place of not just any old skull, but the place of the skull of Goliath of Gath.[19]

Professor Rick Shenk concurs with Marshall and aptly gives context to the magnitude of the battle between David and Goliath and its accompanying ramifications:

This battle was not merely about Philistines and Israelites; it was about who rules over heaven and earth: the Serpent or YHWH! And now comes David, not with Serpent armor or weapons, but with powerful declarations: "this day YHWH will deliver you into my hand, and I will strike you down and cut off your head" (1 Samuel 17:46). That should ring a bell for us! Indeed, David proceeds to bruise Goliath on the head with a stone. The Serpent-warrior fell on his face and ate dust. And then, David removed Goliath's head with his enemy's own sword. In this battle against the Serpent, the seed won! . . . Whether or not Goliath of Gath is the correct etymology of Golgotha, it was in this very city to which the head of Goliath was taken. It was on this very hill where Jesus' feet were pierced by the nails. It was in this very place that he crushed the head of the Serpent.[20]

"It Is Finished"

It would be another one thousand years until Jesus, the Son of David, would triumphantly utter the words "It is finished" (John 19:30 NIV) on Golgotha, the place of the skull. But, during that time span, the seed would pass from David through the generations, ultimately, finally to be brought to life at the perfect time. The apostle Paul describes the miraculous occurrence: "But when the fullness of time had come, God sent his Son, born of a woman" (Gal 4:4 NIV).

19. Marshall, "Golgotha."
20. Shenk, "David and Goliath."

That's why it is so important to read the lineage of Jesus in the Gospels. They are the record of the kingdom-seed of the woman, traveling miraculously through time. God used imperfect, faith-filled people throughout the ages to accomplish his perfect, redemptive plan. The plan that he had prophesied in the garden in Gen 3:14–15. It had come to its full fruition in Jesus. Let's read the list of names. Some will be recognizable and some will not. Some pronounceable and some not. But all of them, set in place and in line, to perfectly release in full force, the serpent-crushing seed to accomplish his eternal work . . .

> "You are my Son, the Beloved; with you I am well pleased." [23] Jesus was about thirty years old when he began his work. He was the son (as was thought) of Joseph son of Heli, [24] son of Matthat, son of Levi, son of Melchi, son of Jannai, son of Joseph, [25] son of Mattathias, son of Amos, son of Nahum, son of Esli, son of Naggai, [26] son of Maath, son of Mattathias, son of Semein, son of Josech, son of Joda, [27] son of Joanan, son of Rhesa, son of Zerubbabel, son of Shealtiel, son of Neri, [28] son of Melchi, son of Addi, son of Cosam, son of Elmadam, son of Er, [29] son of Joshua, son of Eliezer, son of Jorim, son of Matthat, son of Levi, [30] son of Simeon, son of Judah, son of Joseph, son of Jonam, son of Eliakim, [31] son of Melea, son of Menna, son of Mattatha, son of Nathan, son of David, [32] son of Jesse, son of Obed, son of Boaz, son of Sala, son of Nahshon, [33] son of Amminadab, son of Admin, son of Arni, son of Hezron, son of Perez, son of Judah, [34] son of Jacob, son of Isaac, son of Abraham, son of Terah, son of Nahor, [35] son of Serug, son of Reu, son of Peleg, son of Eber, son of Shelah, [36] son of Cainan, son of Arphaxad, son of Shem, son of Noah, son of Lamech, [37] son of Methuselah, son of Enoch, son of Jared, son of Mahalaleel, son of Cainan, [38] son of Enos, son of Seth, son of Adam, son of God. (Luke 2:22b–38 NIV)

The Second Adam

In the perfect timing of God, the seed had been carried through time by the aforementioned individuals. God had used them, through faith, to birth an entirely new race of humanity. A second Adam. An Adam who would not fail. One who would not fall. Never before was there one like him, nor will there ever be again. He is the First and Last of his kind. Solely unique and uniquely sole. The "Alpha and the Omega" (Rev 1:8; 22:31 NIV). For those who will follow him, by faith, there lives an eternal hope, that they, too, through him in them, will live by his life. It will be a new life where *all* things will be "made new" (2 Cor 5:17 NIV). They, too, will crush the serpent all day long and for eternity. Paul gives insight into the mystery of it all:

> The Son is the image of the invisible God, the firstborn over all creation. [16] For in him all things were created: things in heaven and on earth, visible and invisible, whether thrones or powers or rulers or authorities; all things have been created through him and for him. [17] He is before all things, and in him all things hold together. [18] And he is the head of the body, the church; he is the beginning and the firstborn from among the dead, so that in everything he might have the supremacy. [19] For God was pleased to have all his fullness dwell in him, [20] and through him to reconcile to himself all things, whether things on earth or things in heaven, by making peace through his blood, shed on the cross. (Col 1:15–20 NIV)

The Seed was delivered through time for a purpose. He would travel through broken humanity, live on a broken planet, then be impaled on a cross to bleed for the broken. The serpent would strike at his heel, bloodying him. Then, after bleeding on that skull of a rock called Golgotha, for all the world to see, he would declare, "It is finished." A crushing and eternal blow delivered to the serpent's head. The first Adam's penalty, which overshadowed all his children, paid for by the untainted blood of the second. Then, an unexpected (by the serpent) second blow. An eternal nail to death. The crushed serpent, now forever beheaded. Jesus was alive. He had risen from the dead according to the Scriptures. And the crushing would not be only once; it would crush and crush incessantly, forevermore. Paul explains the ramifications of this crushing blow to the serpent and his seed:

> If only for this life we have hope in Christ, we are of all people most to be pitied. [20] But Christ has indeed been raised from the dead, the firstfruits of those who have fallen asleep. For since death came through a man, the resurrection of the dead comes also through a man. [22] For as in Adam all die, so in Christ all will be made alive. (1 Cor 15:19b–22 NIV)

The Seed of the woman, alive forevermore, empowering his followers to live on his behalf. To live and establish serpent-crushing communities all over the world. Communities where the alive, resurrected, serpent-crushing Jesus is the center . . . he is the Thesis. Where individuals set about following a living, serpent-crushing Savior. One who eats with them, teaches them, gives them marching orders, then empowers them to march. Luke, in his Gospel, recounts what Jesus instructing and empowering the first communities looked like:

> After his suffering, he presented himself to them and gave many convincing proofs that he was alive. He appeared to them over a period of forty days and spoke about the kingdom of God. [4] On one occasion, while he was eating with them, he gave them this command: "Do not leave Jerusalem, but wait for the gift my Father promised, which you have heard me speak about. [5] For John baptized with water, but in a few days you will be baptized with the Holy Spirit." [6] Then they gathered around him and asked him, "Lord, are you at this time going to restore the kingdom to Israel?" [7] He said to them: "It is not for you to know the times or dates the Father has set by his own authority. [8] But you will receive power when the Holy Spirit comes on you; and you will be my witnesses in Jerusalem, and in all Judea and Samaria, and to the ends of the earth." (Acts 1:3–8 NIV)

The Seed crushes the serpent, then bestows his crushing power to his people, enabling them to defeat death and bring life. Through the Holy Spirit, Christ empowers his followers to live as he did, to die as he did, and to rise as he did. It is the Thesis himself and his life, death, and resurrection to whom we now turn.

Part 3

The Thesis Himself

Like all of creation, the world has been created through Christ and toward Christ and has its existence only in Christ (John 1:10; Col. 1:16). To speak of the world without speaking of Christ is pure abstraction.

—DIETRICH BONHOEFFER, *ETHICS*[1]

Who Is Christ?

THE ONE WHO HOLDS everything together, who existed before time, yet entered into it. He became human, lived a holy life—healing the sick, caring for the poor. He died a brutal death, one of self-giving love, conquering death itself. He rose again, freeing humanity from the bond of sin. This is the story of Jesus of Nazareth. This is the story of the one true God. This is the story we get to enter, because he entered into ours.

1. Bonhoeffer, *Ethics*, 19.

7

The Kenotic King

THERE IS NO BEGINNING for the story of Jesus. There was an entrance—a birth, an incarnation—but no beginning. Before Jesus was born, he was. In the words of the Gospel of John:

> In the beginning was the Word, and the Word was with God, and the Word was God. [2] He was in the beginning with God. [3] All things came into being through him, and without him not one thing came into being. What has come into being [4] in him was life, and the life was the light of all people. [5] The light shines in the darkness, and the darkness did not overcome it. (John 1:1–5)

The Word, the one through whom all things came into being, who existed when the universe itself was created, is Jesus of Nazareth. This idea of Jesus being God, existing before the earth's foundations, was not clear to his disciples in the early years. They all, surely, had their unique ideas of who this guy was—a great teacher, a political leader, even a Messiah. The everlasting God, though? It probably took a while to occur to them. He was Jesus, their friend. After his resurrection from the dead, though, they had to figure it out. They had to ask themselves, what did all this mean? And how should it affect their everyday lives? They met an unimaginable event. The next step was to assess its meaning and tell people about it. The Gospels are a product of that process. These Gospels, which make up almost half of the New Testament, were attempts by the authors to explain the meaning of the life, death, and resurrection of Jesus. These aren't rote, lifeless biographies but sincere attempts amid life's difficulties and doubts to find the meaning in these cataclysmic events.

John's introduction is a beautiful example of this endeavor, drawing from multiple traditions to explain the divine nature of a man from Nazareth. He weaves this explanation with strands of divine language used in both Jewish and Greek theology and philosophy. To write of Jesus in his prologue, John refers to Jesus as the Word. In Stoic philosophy, the Word or *Logos* was the ordering principle of the universe. The Stoic ethic arises from a desire to live in harmony with that order. While hinting at this Greek *Logos*, John directly alludes to a feature of Jewish theology and its wisdom tradition.

In Ps 104:24, we see the psalmist praising God for creating "in wisdom." In Prov 8, we see this Wisdom personified, taking an active part in that creative process, saying, "When he established the heavens, I was there" (8:27). Throughout the Hebrew Bible, Wisdom is in the background, an agent of God working to bring life—"the personified word of Yahweh."[1] This idea gains steam in the period between what we call the Old and New Testaments. In a Jewish writing during that time called Wisdom of Solomon, Wisdom reveals the nature of the world. Not only that, but Wisdom is "a breath of the power of God, and a pure emanation of the glory of the Almighty . . . a reflection of eternal light, a spotless mirror of the working of God, and an image of his goodness" (Wis 7:25–26). Interestingly, in Sirach (24), Wisdom comes to dwell among humanity in the temple. Taken all together, the Jewish tradition sees Wisdom as the personification of God's creative power, bringer of life, revealer of God, a perfect reflection of his goodness.

John draws from these traditions—Wisdom and *Logos*—to bring to mind a powerful, divine, creative, and good being: a being who brings life and harmony, who existed before the foundations of the earth and will continue to exist for eternity. This being is the one through whom we know what is true and beautiful, who is the revelation of the God of the universe. He then tells us that being is Jesus of Nazareth. The guy his readers heard about, the son of Mary and Joseph, the rebel who preached and healed and died on a cross—that man is the preexistent Christ. "The word became flesh and lived among us, and we have seen his glory, the glory as of a father's only son, full of grace and truth" (John 1:14).

---

1. Wright and Bird, *New Testament*, 664.

Incarnation

It may seem an odd question, but how many times have you washed your hands in the last week? How often do you have to wipe down a counter, vacuum your floors, brush your teeth? The human experience is a messy one. It requires us to do maintenance, to keep things clean: not to mention the existential messiness—the anxieties and the pains. It's no wonder we tend to escape to virtual spaces. It *is* a wonder, though, that the divine being John spoke of—the one through whom all things came into being—chose to take on that human experience, filth and all. He wrote, "And the Word became flesh and lived among us" (1:14a). That divine being chose to live among its creation, as one of them. He took on the human experience, including the most vulnerable parts. He even came as a child, wholly and utterly dependent on another.

The incarnation is at once a surprise and completely unsurprising. Nobody quite expected God to do it, but it is in his nature to incarnate. Throughout the Old Testament, God desired to be with humanity. He walked in the garden of Eden. He dwelled in the temple. He called to Moses out of a burning bush. He appeared in cloud and fire to guide his people. Drawing on the "self-emptying," or *kenosis*, of Christ in Phil 2, New Testament scholar Michael Gorman writes, "The servant-like, kenotic activities attributed to Christ in 2:6–8 are in fact divine in character, or to put it the other way around, divinity has kenotic servanthood as its essential attribute."[2] This is far from the detached deistic gods we tend to imagine—gods who create and then wait and see how things turn out, intervening only for their own benefit. The God of the Christian faith, the God become human in Jesus, is one who cares deeply for his creation, who constantly and unceasingly desires to be with them, to care for them, to love them. So much so that, as Paul writes, "He did not regard equality with God as something to be exploited, but emptied himself, taking the form of a slave, being born in human likeness" (Phil 2:6b–7).

There are two aspects to this movement that are important for us to notice. The first is that it is a movement of humility, a coming down to care for those in need. It's a movement that refuses to exploit the privilege one has for their own gain but instead pursues the good of the other. Rather than grasping at power, it embraces the powerless. It's a movement inherent in the God of the universe and instantiated in the person of Jesus Christ.

2. Gorman, *Inhabiting the Cruciform God*, 31.

This means that, for the Christian faith, this is an essential movement—an essential posture. In the Philippians passage, the message is that God is this way, so you should be this way. Not only that, but because God is this way, he gives you the power to be. The *kenosis* of God enables our *kenotic* activity. While we don't often live up to it, we are to be a "self-emptying" people. Fortunately, even when we fail, our God continues his humble activity, loving us unceasingly.

The second aspect of this movement that is important for us to notice is the value it places on that which God becomes. While we often desire to escape the physical—retreating to digital, or even spiritual, unembodied spaces—God works in the reverse. He created a world he called good, a human people he called very good, and he reaffirms that claim by taking the form of his creation. In coming down to it, he elevated it. The human experience is not one to be escaped but to be embraced. The human body, even, is not one to be escaped but to be embraced. It's not weighing us down, as ironic as that might feel. When God took human form, it was an unambiguous affirmation of physical reality, messiness and all. While by no means the only application of this concept,[3] this does lead us to a sort of Christocentric body positivity. While pop psychology provides aphoristic calls to accept your body no matter its shape, one can't help but feel an emptiness in those words. Yet if the God who created that body affirms it, we can't help but call it good. That doesn't mean it's perfect (we may need to be healthier in one way or another), but it does mean it is valuable, made for a purpose, and loved by the God of the universe.

There's a reason Christmas is a significant holiday in the Christian tradition. It celebrates the birth of Christ, the incarnation of God. It's an act filled with meaning these simple words could not express—revealing a God ever moving toward his people, seeking solidarity with them, desiring their good, and as we will see soon, with them in their pain. In the words of Jürgen Moltmann, "The God who has become human has made our lives part of his life, and our sufferings his suffering."[4]

---

3. Another vitally important application is what some call "creation care." This world has been given to us and is valued by our Creator. Caring for it is not a partisan act but a moral one—in keeping with the Christian ethic.

4. Moltmann, *Jesus Christ for Today's World*, 45.

Words and Deeds

It may be an obvious thing to write, but Jesus didn't go straight from birth to death. As we mentioned earlier, a large part of the New Testament, the Gospels, fill us in on that. He did so much more than arrive and die. He taught, he healed, he performed the miraculous. We find in the Gospels, though, that all of this was in service of announcing the kingdom. What this kingdom is and how it changes the world it encounters is essential to understanding who Jesus is—and through that, what he means for the world. From Moltmann again: "For who is Jesus? *Simply the kingdom of God in person.*"[5]

Announcing the Kingdom

Let's start with the beginning of Jesus's ministry. After the genealogies and birth narratives, baptisms and temptations, the Gospels all portray the beginning of Jesus's ministry in fascinating ways, each emblematic of the kind of work the Gospel is doing. They were all written in relatively hostile environments in which they advocated for their new way of life, preaching about a new kingdom in which they were taking part. The Gospel of Matthew portrays the beginning of Jesus's ministry in just this way. After his lengthy early remarks regarding the genealogy of Jesus, his birth, baptism, and temptation, Matthew wrote, "From that time Jesus began to proclaim, 'Repent, for the kingdom of heaven has come near'" (Matt 4:17). According to Matthew, that is the message of Jesus, the good news he's telling—the kingdom of heaven has come near. In Mark, we get a nearly identical start to the ministry of Jesus. (Although Mark arrives much faster. Matthew is much wordier.) He wrote, "Jesus came to Galilee, proclaiming the good news of God, and saying, 'The time is fulfilled, and the kingdom of God has come near; repent, and believe in the good news'" (Mark 1:14b–15). In Luke, we get something a little different. In his recounting of the start of Jesus's ministry, he gives us a few more words from Jesus himself. Luke tells us Jesus began traveling and preaching in synagogues throughout the area. When Jesus gets to Nazareth, he gets up to speak, unrolls a scroll of Isaiah, and reads:

---

5. Moltmann, *Jesus Christ for Today's World*, 7 (emphasis in original).

The Spirit of the Lord is upon me,
because he has anointed me
to bring good news to the poor.
He has sent me to proclaim release to the captives
and recovery of sight to the blind,
to let the oppressed go free,
[19] to proclaim the year of the Lord's favor. (Luke 4:18–19)

Jesus then rolls up the scroll and sits down. As all the synagogue's eyes remain fixed on him, he says, "Today this Scripture has been fulfilled in your hearing" (Luke 4:21). Apparently, this is what the kingdom is about. It's good news for the poor; it's about releasing those who are captive, curing those who are ill, and freeing those who are oppressed. The good news of Jesus is not a prayer you have to pray or a moral failing you have to fix. The good news of Jesus is that he is good, and he brings a new way of life with him. All we have to do is get on board, join him in his world-changing work, and proclaim along with him this hope for those who need it. And Jesus doesn't just say this, but as you read the rest of these Gospels, you see him carrying out this kingdom work.

Healing the Sick

There are many for whom sickness and pain are constant companions. There are none for whom sickness and pain are altogether absent. The reality is we are all fragile creatures, one moment away from needing help. These experiences are ubiquitous, and while the world God created is certainly good, suffering is certainly not.

The Gospel of John tells the story of a man born blind, whom Jesus encounters on the road. His disciples ask him, "Who sinned, this man or his parents, that he was born blind?" (John 9:2) Our modern tendency would be to balk at this question and the superstition of such a remark. Yet take away the religious connotations and we are not much different. The sick are a burden, the disabled a weight we don't want to carry. It's not our responsibility to care for them. While they may not be to blame, neither are we.

Jesus corrects their remark, noting that the question of blame is misguided. Neither is to blame. However, it does provide an opportunity for the "works of God" to be revealed in him. What are these "works of God"? They are works that make people whole—by curing disease and recognizing the humanity of the suffering. Jesus refuses to lay the blame on the blind man. He also refuses to let him go unhelped, taking on the responsibility of caring for him. The kingdom of God, then, is one where the assigning of blame is ditched and replaced by the carrying of each other's burdens—the real, physical burdens of those in our community. Jesus is not just concerned with the "saving of souls" but the restoration of the whole person. "In healing the sick, the kingdom takes bodily form."[6]

We pride ourselves in our technological achievements, our medical advancements, our political progress, yet all the while, people are still hungry, the sick are still uncared for—and we go on with our lives, numbing ourselves to other people's suffering. There's a reason the healing of the sick is such a prominent part of Jesus's ministry. Jesus refuses to be numbed, welcoming those who come to him in need, offering hope that there will be an end to the pain. In sickness, we are reminded of our frailty, and in healing, we are reminded of our hope. Through Christ, all will be healed. There is no one he will ignore. Come to him and he will give you life, life abundant. The kingdom of God is one where people are made whole, where dignity is restored, where the blind are given sight.

Welcoming the Outcast

The fifth chapter of Luke tells a few short stories that speak to how Jesus cares for the downtrodden, the outcast, and the shunned. The first occurs when Jesus sees two boats on the shore of a lake. The fisherman had fished all night and caught nothing. Down on their luck, they were washing their nets and packing up for the night. Jesus tells them to send their boat back into deep water and let their nets down again. Somewhat reluctantly, they agree. They had fished all night and caught nothing. Why go out again? This time, though, when they cast out their nets, they begin to break under the weight of the fish. After calling for help, they filled both boats that night. They bring them to shore and decide right then to follow Jesus, becoming part of his closest twelve disciples. This miracle seems somewhat mundane compared to the healings we see throughout the Gospels. We don't get any indication that they would starve without that catch.[7] Yet Jesus still chooses to intervene. There's something beautiful about that mundane provision, that moment where Jesus notices and cares. He sees those in need and won't

---

6. Moltmann, *Jesus Christ for Today's World*, 13.

7. Although they probably weren't far from it. Given the drastic inequities of the time, many of Jesus's followers, and Jesus himself, were most likely living at subsistence levels.

pass them by. He cares for this group of fishermen, down on their luck, and gives them the catch of their lives. Jesus teaches to pray, in the Lord's Prayer, "Give us this day our daily bread." And here we see him doing just that, providing for the everyday necessities of a person's life.

The second story we read in this chapter is of a man with a skin disease. This disease resulted in the man being considered unclean and excluded from society.[8] When Jesus saw him, the man cried out, "Lord, if you choose, you can make me clean." Jesus then stretched out his hand and touched him, saying, "I do choose. Be made clean." Luke notes, "Immediately the skin disease left him" (Luke 5:12–13). The man's faith is worth mentioning here, as he comes to Jesus, recognizing his lordship. Jesus is not just the one heralding the coming kingdom; he is that kingdom's king. Fortunately, Jesus is not like any other king, which is why this language is so tricky.

The word *kingdom* is foreign to our largely democratic sentiments and our autonomous ideals. As Americans especially, we value the rogue, the maverick, the Wild West—free from authority, free from control. This sentiment shouldn't be jettisoned immediately. Given human nature, authority is often twisted, cruel, and abusive. Many of us have good reason to question and resist authority, as many of us have been mistreated in the past, which is what makes "king" and "kingdom" problematic. Like every human designation, they come with spoiled connotations. When our experience of authority comes with abuse, a word like king, the ultimate kind of authority, will undoubtedly be marred. We see in passages like this, though, that this king is not like any other. The man calls out, "If you choose . . ." and Jesus responds, "I do choose." Jesus chooses to heal; he desires that all be cured, all barriers to acceptance into loving community be removed. The kingdom of God is not like any other kingdom, and Jesus is not like any other king.

Before his crucifixion, Jesus is on trial before Pilate, the Roman governor of the area. He's on trial for his claims of authority, some calling him king of the Jews. Pilate asks him, "Are you the king of the Jews?" He responds, "You say so." This response puts the words back on Pilate. Jesus isn't claiming to be king; others are calling him such. This answer is also fascinating in that, in response to being asked if he is a king, it's as if he says, "Well, that's your word for it."[9] King, like any human language applied to

---

8. "Luke's hearers understand the sparse description of leprosy as a skin disorder (not Hansen's disease) that required heartrending exclusion from normal society (Lev. 13:46; Josephus *Ant.* 3.264: 'as good as dead')" (Brawley, "Jesus and Christian Gospels," 225).

9. This thought is borrowed from a couple tweets by New Testament scholar Laura Robinson. See Robinson, "There's a live possibility."

God, is analogical. It can't fully grasp or explain what God is like, but it can point us to something while pulling us beyond it. Jesus isn't a king in the way we think of kings. He is far more and far better.

We see this through stories like the ones Luke tells in his Gospel. Stories like providing fish for those down on their luck or curing and welcoming a diseased and outcast man. Jesus brings a new kingdom, one where the hungry are fed, the sick are healed, and the one left out is lovingly brought in. That's because Jesus's kingdom, unlike any other kingdom before or after, is *for* those people.

Teaching about the Kingdom

Shortly after these stories of miracle and healing, Luke recounts Jesus teaching in front of a crowd. The first line of this sermon is, "Blessed are you who are poor, for yours is the kingdom of God" (Luke 6:20). He goes on to announce blessings to all kinds of people in need—those who are hungry, those who weep, those who are hated. He then announces "woes," proclamations of grief or distress, beginning with "Woe to you who are rich, for you have received your consolation" (Luke 6:24). In talking about salvation in Christ, we tend to spiritualize it, disembody it, and kick it to the afterlife. This misses vital aspects of what Jesus taught and did. First, while the afterlife is an essential component of the kingdom (where all of this will be completed), the work has already begun, and Jesus is inviting all to join in. Those who follow Christ aren't just hoping for a great future but participating in bringing that future into reality here and now. Second, Jesus didn't just preach forgiveness of sins but also healing for the sick and freedom for the oppressed. The kingdom of God, while certainly spiritual, is not *merely* spiritual. It is meant to be brought to bear on the embodied realities of human lives.

There's a moment in the Gospels where John the Baptist begins to doubt whether Jesus is the Messiah, the "anointed one" prophesied to bring about God's redemption of the world. It's a fascinating moment, especially given John's role in announcing and baptizing Jesus. John had surely experienced some arduous moments since that time, currently imprisoned for speaking out against Herod, the area's ruler. And in those moments, he wondered, "Was I right? Is Jesus really the Messiah?" So he sends a messenger from prison to ask Jesus, "Are you the Messiah, the one who was to come? Or should we wait for another?" Jesus tells him, "Go and tell John what you hear and see: the blind receive their sight, the lame walk, the lepers are cleansed, the deaf hear, the dead are raised, and the poor have good news brought to them" (Matt 11:4–5). According to Jesus, the evidence that the kingdom of God has come is that the physical realities of people in need are altered.

Another way to say all of this is that Jesus cares about justice. If a person being set right is made righteous, a society set right is made just, and Jesus came to do it all. He brings good news not only to sinners but also to victims of sin[10]—desiring not only to restore our relationships with God but also with each other. Similar to the numerous other ways in which Jesus is different from every other king, his justice is different too. It refuses to give rise to hatred. Instead, following these proclamations of blessing and woe, he gives commands to love your enemies and turn the other cheek (Luke 6:27–31)—a response that seeks to give to each what they need, rather than what they deserve. As we'll see in the following chapter, Jesus models this exact kind of self-sacrificial love, even unto death. It's a love he calls all of us to, inviting us into this way of the kingdom of God, lifting up the oppressed, calling out the oppressor, and providing a path forward—ending the cycle of injustice by embracing unconditional love.

The Anxiety of Christ

On the night of his arrest, Jesus ventured out with a few of his disciples to a garden called Gethsemane, at the Mount of Olives. He went there to pray. Knowing what was to come—his arrest, betrayal, torture, execution—he entered in anguish. Two of the Gospels note that he was "grieved and agitated" (Matt 26:37, Mark 14:33). Luke paints us a dismal picture, writing, "In his anguish he prayed more earnestly, and his sweat became like great drops of blood falling down on the ground" (Luke 22:44). Jesus approached these events not as someone taken by surprise, but with full knowledge of what he was about to experience. He was in control. Yet, at the same time, he was anxious. He dreaded what was to come. This is a remarkable moment in the story of God. If it's true that Jesus is who we've claimed him to be, then this is a moment where the God of the universe—who set the universe into motion, who spoke the stars into existence, who gave life to each and every one of us—experienced anxiety. He saw what was before him and felt

---

10. This phrasing is borrowed from a podcast interview. See Martinez-Olivieri, "Jules Martinez-Olivieri."

the chill of dread. His muscles tensed, his heart beat faster, he felt that pain deep in the stomach. He experienced that sensation of replaying the pain that hasn't yet arrived, hoping for a way out. We've all felt it. God felt it too.

One might want to soften this description, to preserve Jesus's idyllic divinity, but the Gospels don't. They even note that he prayed, "Father, if you are willing, remove this cup from me; yet, not my will but yours be done" (Luke 22:42). Matthew records Jesus praying this prayer three times (Matt 26:39–44):

> Father, if you are willing, remove this cup from me; yet, not my will but yours be done.

This is an incredible detail because it reveals to us both that Jesus was wholly obedient—even unto death, for our sake—while also experiencing acute dread regarding that decision. We are the ones in need of salvation, yet he enters into our dread to bring us up from it. This is not a weakening of his divinity, but rather reveals to us true divinity's nature. It enters into the suffering of others, lives there with them, in hopes to eventually bring them out of it. This is the *kenosis* of Christ written about in Phil 2. The movement made at the beginning of the Gospels, where the preexistent Christ incarnates for our sake, is the same movement made at the end of the Gospels, where the incarnate Christ takes on the suffering of the world to the point of death. As Gorman writes, "The divine one emptied himself by becoming a slave, becoming human. So, too, the human one humbled himself by becoming obedient to death."[11]

Anxiety tends to separate us, isolate us, into ourselves and away from others. We feel alone in it, controlled by it, and without hope of conquering it. Yet in our anxiety, Christ is with us. By holding onto an idyllic divinity, some miss the hope brought on by a God who suffers with us. Moltmann writes, "By recognizing our fear in his, and by seeing our fear as caught up in his, we experience that 'blessed anxiety' (as Georges Bernanos called it) which kindles an unconquerable hope."[12]

Jesus is God-become-human, healer of the sick, liberator of the oppressed, who welcomes the outcast and brings good news to the poor. He makes the mundane sacred and, by suffering with us, brings hope to our anxiety. Ultimately, he is a *kenotic* king. He's the one who rules the world, yet always and forever gives himself for it.

---

11. Gorman, *Inhabiting the Cruciform God*, 22.

12. Moltmann, *Jesus Christ for Today's World*, 57.

8

For Our Sake

"FOR OUR SAKE HE was crucified under Pontius Pilate, he suffered death and was buried." These words are taken from the Nicene Creed, a staple among Christians for over 1700 years.[1] What it means that Jesus was crucified "for our sake" is a lot to unpack, and we'll get to that. Before we do, though, we don't want to brush over the rest of this statement. While it is only a small portion of the larger creed, there is a wealth of meaning jam-packed into these few words—meaning that can give life and bring hope to even the worst of our suffering. We'll take it from end to beginning.

He Suffered Death

Given what we have covered so far, this is a remarkable statement. God suffered death. In Genesis, after Adam and Eve took the fruit from the forbidden tree, God lays out the consequences of that act. In the culmination of this poetic response, God tells the man he will die—"You are dust, and to dust you shall return" (Gen 3:19b). In Ash Wednesday services around the world, Christians yearly remember this phrase. After having ashes placed on their forehead, they are told, "Remember that you are dust, and to dust you shall return." This is an inescapable truth of human reality. Death is inevitable. We can run from it. We can ignore it. It will still come for us.

---

1. The Nicene Creed as most use it today is actually the Niceno-Constantinopolitan creed. The creed was issued at the First Council of Constantinople but it shares many similarities with the creed issued at the earlier First Council of Nicaea. For a brief overview of this, see Britannica, "Nicene Creed." See also Gonzalez, *Story of Christianity*, chs. 17 and 20.

For us, death is inevitable; but for him, it was not. That is what makes this statement remarkable. Jesus did not have to die. He could have forgone incarnation, he could have left us in our sorry state. Yet he didn't. Back to Phil 2, "being found in human form, he humbled himself, and became obedient to the point of death—even death on a cross" (2:7-8). He took on that dust and carried it to its inevitable demise.

The phrasing "He suffered death" could have been simply stated "He died." But no, death is not that simple. It comes with all kinds of other pains. It comes with anxiety, uncertainty, and dread. Death is a form of cutting off, becoming separated from life itself and every other being possessing that life. He *suffered* death. Jesus, in one of the few recorded phrases from him on the cross, says, "My God, my God, why have you forsaken me?" In his dying, he enters the depths of human suffering and cries out in a deeply human refrain. These words he speaks are taken from Ps 22, where it continues, "Why are you so far from helping me, from the words of my groaning? O my God, I cry by day, but you do not answer; and by night, but find no rest" (Ps 22:1-2). This is the problem of evil in a nutshell. If God exists, where is he when we suffer? When I cry for help, is he listening?

The glibness with which many Christians respond to that question exposes their inattention to this moment. This moment where Christ is crying out in pain, feeling the weight of despair, and his followers are looking up to the cross, their leader defeated. When we begin to sit with this moment of Christ on the cross, seemingly Godforsaken, we recognize that our pat answers and pithy retorts do little for a person entering the depths of human despair. We would do well to remember that the Bible never gives an easy answer to human suffering. When encountering suffering, an answer is rarely the solution anyway. Propositional knowledge is largely unhelpful in this sphere. What a person needs is relationship and new habits of mind. Not facts but new ways of thinking—and people to take the journey with us. What we see in the cross is God joining the suffering with us. He takes it upon himself. While this doesn't give us an answer to suffering, it does reveal that God is not exempt from it. He does not leave us to suffer alone. So rather than giving an answer to suffering, God embraces it. He looks deep into it and, at the very last moment—like breath on cooling embers—fans hope into a flame. Jurgen Moltmann writes, "Why God permits all this we do not know. And if we did know, it would not help us to live. But if we discover where God is, and sense his presence in our suffering, then we are at the fountainhead—the source out of which life is born anew."[2]

Moltmann's words here come from vivid experience. He recounts a moment in a prisoner of war camp at the end of World War II, feeling the great weight of abandonment, by God and humanity. He was handed a Bible by an American soldier and began to read it. He was "drawn to the story of the passion, and when [he] came to Jesus' death cry [he] knew: this is the one who understands you and is beside you when everyone else abandons you." His words are worth including in full:

> "My God, why have you forsaken me?" That was my cry for God too. I began to understand the suffering, assailed and God-forsaken Jesus, because I felt that he understood me. And I grasped that this Jesus is the divine Brother in our distress. He brings hope to the prisoners and the abandoned. He is the one who delivers us from the guilt that weighs us down and robs us of every kind of future. And I became possessed by a hope when in human terms there was little enough to hope for. I summoned up the courage to live, at a point when one would perhaps willingly have put an end to it all. This early companionship with Jesus, the brother in suffering and the liberator from guilt, has never left me since. The Christ for me is the crucified Jesus.[3]

Under Pontius Pilate

The death of Jesus is not mere story, mere myth, but myth become fact. The Nicene Creed expresses this truth in the inclusion of this rather minor historical character, Pontius Pilate. He was the Roman governor of Judea and would be discussed little, if not for that it was under his governance that Jesus was executed. Pilate grounds the creed, and Jesus's death, in history. He reminds us that the death of Jesus is not merely a story to comfort us. (Although it certainly should.) It is a historical reality, with historical consequences that must be reckoned with. Jesus is not a generic hero open to endless rebranding but a flesh and blood person who struggled against flesh and blood power. We may at times want to lift him out of the pages of history and worship him simply as a figure of love and peace. Yet while that may feel like an expansion of his message, it is in fact a reduction. That

2. Moltmann, *Jesus Christ for Today's World*, 46.
3. Moltmann, *Jesus Christ for Today's World*, 2–3.

amorphous Jesus can do little for those in the thick of life's complexity. That Jesus can do little for those struggling against oppressive political powers. The Jesus of history, the one crucified under Pontius Pilate, is a Jesus for the suffering. Kelly Brown Douglas notes that this identification with the suffering is "much more than an impassive identification with those least regarded in society. The crucifixion unquestionably reveals a *compassionate solidarity* with them. Jesus is *with* the powerless in their very dehumanizing condition, even to the point of crucifixion."[4]

The creed includes Pilate, as Paul S. Fiddes has noted, "to make clear that God's saving act has happened right in the middle of the human politics of power and fear."[5] By spiritualizing, or rather dematerializing Jesus, we forget the ways in which his death was a confrontation not only with death, but with the powers that bring it. These powers—of false religion, corrupt government, and the like—use fear to ensnare and strangle, to fuel their power, and they are confronted by the Jesus of history. The events precipitating his execution reveal this rebel Jesus. Rebel, not in our colloquial usage, but its proper form. While his crucifixion was certainly unjust, it was not without cause. Crucifixion was a method of punishment used by the Roman government for "people of low status, slaves, violent criminals, and rebels who threatened and opposed Rome's rule."[6] Jesus was crucified because he fit that last category. It's noted in every Gospel that his charge was placed in an inscription above his head, "This is Jesus, King of the Jews" (Matt 27:37, Mark 15:26, Luke 23:38, John 19:19). He was killed because he claimed to be the true king of all. He claimed to have authority no one else had. He was killed because he was establishing a kingdom—a kingdom for the oppressed. By over-spiritualizing Jesus's death, we over-spiritualize its effects. By grounding Jesus in history, we realize there is far more he set out to do. His death is not just about the forgiveness of sins and bringing eternal life; it's a confrontation with evil itself and the numerous ways it manifests to enslave us here and now.

By ignoring the historical reality, we also forget how truly counterintuitive the death of Christ was. In 1 Corinthians, Paul writes that the cross is "foolishness to those who are perishing, but to those who are being saved it is the power of God" (1:18). In the first-century world, a faith based on a person who was crucified was indeed by all accounts foolish. The Jews

4. Douglas, *What's Faith Got*, ch. 3.
5. Fiddes, *Past Event*, 35.
6. Warren, *Seven Events*, 94.

believed that anyone crucified was cursed, and given the kind of person who was crucified, everyone else would have simply written them off as a criminal, often of the worst kind. That a movement sprung up with such vigor after the crucifixion of their leader is truly bizarre, and Paul here is addressing that, acknowledging the "foolishness" of it. What Paul argues here, though, is that this seeming foolishness is in fact the "power of God." Somehow, in the death of Christ, the power of God is revealed.

That the church took time to remember the death of Christ, and continues to do so, is truly remarkable. The death of Jesus was a failure. A failure of justice and a failure of the movement. Yet churches all over the world take time every week to remember it, in one of our most blessed sacraments—the Eucharist. The reason for this is captured in Paul's description of its foolishness. While it is foolish, it is also the power of God, because the power of God is found in his weakness. Just like the ever-self-emptying nature of God is revealed in the incarnation, so it is revealed in his death. God is not one to overpower. Rather, he draws us in through weakness. He accomplishes his works not by force but by self-sacrifice. The political and religious powers of our world achieve their ends through the coercion of others. By addressing those powers head-on, to the point of death, Jesus exposes them for what they are—empty, corrupt, bringing death to the innocent. It is in Jesus's obedience to death that we see his exaltation as true King, the one who will liberate us all. Jesus suffered under Pontius Pilate, and in doing so, he brought hope to those suffering under all kinds of oppressive forces.

For Our Sake

When Jesus died, then rose again, it ignited a movement. Much of the New Testament writings, and those that came after, were attempts to make sense of those events. They all had a sense that Jesus's death was "for our sake." So much so that three hundred years later, those words appeared in the creed. The meaning of Jesus's death "for our sake" has been debated since these first Christian writings, and analogy after analogy has been used to attempt to explain it, some more adequate than others. The overarching theme is that the death and resurrection of Jesus somehow reconcile God and humanity. The word for this reconciliation is *atonement*. There are some explanations of atonement taking into account the sacrificial themes of the Hebrew Bible; some are more oriented toward legal codes and God's sense of justice, some appeal to the moral force of the death of Jesus as a way forward for human life, and there are many others.[7] What these theories have in common is that humanity has a serious problem, and Jesus, through his death and resurrection, provides a solution. Given our tendency toward violence, toward oppression, toward injustice generally, that there is a problem with humanity is difficult to deny. Even if one doesn't buy the traditional Genesis story, that we are "fallen" is evident. And if not fallen from some previous whole state, we are certainly capable of more.[8] The claim of Christianity is that the death and resurrection of Jesus provide a way for us to be made whole again—to be reconciled with our God and each other.

As scientific people, assessing the process of humanity's reconciliation to God is difficult. We want to know the exact mechanism for this event to take place. We don't just want to know *that* it is happening but *how*. Unfortunately, our scientific minds are incapable of grasping the infinite. There is much in the world of theology that is not quite in our grasp. We can reach for it, we can create analogies and thought experiments—but when all is said and done, our language is imperfect. We're always going to come up short. So it is with this particular topic. There is a reason there is so much disagreement on the atonement. There is a reason each era focuses on a different, sometimes new, theory. We're all attempting to explain a mysterious yet world-changing event with imperfect language and an incomplete grasp of the reality. Theology is not the only place where this problem exists, though. Try explaining the mechanics of love or beauty, and you'll find you come up woefully short. Poets and artists can gesture toward their enduring reality, illicit their corresponding feelings, but no philosopher, psychologist, or scientist can completely explain them. So it is with the death and resurrection of Christ. One can know it affects them, that it is eternally significant, and still not be able to explain it fully. While all of this is true, there is still value in the attempt. Each attempt brings more light—more light to help us see the truth and beauty of Jesus Christ.

So what about the death of Jesus works toward the reconciliation mentioned above? To give a whole answer to that question, one needs the

7. Paul S. Fiddes provides a charitable and helpful overview of many of these theories, grounding them in their historical context. See *Past Event*, ch. 1.

8. This is one often neglected truth in the doctrine of the fall. To deny that we are somehow depraved as a human species is to deny that there is more that we could be. In reality, the fall should give us hope that there is more to our often sorry reality. We can, in truth, hope for an end to our present injustices, because we were made for something better.

response of resurrection, but that's a topic for the next chapter. For the rest of this discussion, a partial answer must suffice—Jesus's death is for us because it includes us.

Jesus's death includes us in a couple ways. The first way is that, in taking on human form, Jesus transforms humanity itself. In God's infinite perfection, he transforms all he encounters. In taking on anxiety, he transforms it. Now in taking on death, he transforms it. When death takes a loved one, there is an overwhelming sense of separation. While their memory remains, their presence does not. Yet the infinite, ever-present God enters into that death and, through it, conquers separation itself. Through the presence of God, every human is brought near. While death is still certainly a great loss, it is not without hope. In every crevice of our existence, God is there, redeeming it. As Catholic theologian Karl Rahner puts it,

> [Christ] has accepted death. Therefore this must be more than merely a descent into empty meaninglessness. He has accepted the state of being forsaken. Therefore the overpowering sense of loneliness must still contain hidden within itself the promise of God's blessed nearness. He has accepted total failure. Therefore defeat can be a victory. He has accepted abandonment by God. Therefore God is near even when we believe ourselves to have been abandoned by him. He has accepted all things. Therefore all things are redeemed.[9]

Second, in his taking on our life and death, we can through faith participate in his. Michael Gorman argues, in *Inhabiting the Cruciform God*, that this is what Paul imagines justification (or being set right with God and others) to be—"justification is by crucifixion, specifically co-crucifixion, understood as participation in Christ's act of covenant fulfillment."[10] Paul understood Christ as fulfilling the covenant set out by God for the Jewish people—a covenant encapsulated in the twin commands to love God and love one's neighbor—and that we are reconciled to God and to others through participation in his covenant-fulfilling work, crucifixion. For us, this is a metaphorical crucifixion, lived out through literal acts of self-denial, of love for neighbor. While metaphorical, it is grounded in the very real self-sacrifice of Christ on the cross. Our faith in Christ (or allegiance to him) allows us to participate in his covenant-fulfilling act. This is why Paul is able to write in 2 Corinthians, "We are afflicted in every way, but not

9. Karl Rahner, as quoted in Green, *All Things Beautiful*, 102.

10. Gorman, *Inhabiting the Cruciform God*, 43–44.

crushed; perplexed, but not driven to despair; persecuted, but not forsaken; struck down, but not destroyed; always carrying in the body the death of Jesus, so that the life of Jesus may also be made visible in our bodies. For while we live, we are always being given up to death for Jesus' sake, so that the life of Jesus may be made visible in our mortal flesh" (2 Cor 4:8–11). This is exactly why Paul relays the *kenosis* passage to the Philippians. He encourages his readers to "do nothing from selfish ambition or conceit, but in humility regard others as better than yourselves. Let each of you look not to your own interests, but to the interests of others. Let the same mind be in you that was in Christ Jesus" (Phil 2:1–5). The *kenosis* was the mind of Christ, and it is now to be our mind too. It is by participating in his death that we are reconciled to him. And not only to him but to our neighbors. The death of Christ shows us how to live, while at the same time giving us the power to live that way. As Paul says, "I have been crucified with Christ; and it is no longer I who live, but it is Christ who lives in me." (Gal 2:19b–20a) Through the death of Christ, humanity is not only forgiven for sins but liberated from the power of sin.[11] While focused on Christ, this is an imminently Trinitarian picture. We are reconciled to God the Father, through the obedience of the Son, whom we are joined with in a cruciform life, by the power of the Holy Spirit in us.

Lastly, it's important to note, for those who want to become more like Christ, that Jesus on the cross is essential for understanding who he is. An intriguing feature of the Gospel of Mark is that, throughout the life of Jesus, no human speaks to his being the Son of God. This core aspect of Jesus's identity is not spoken to by any human. That is, until he dies. The first announcement of Jesus being the Son of God comes from a Roman soldier standing next to the cross. When he sees Jesus breathe his last breath, he says, "Truly this man was God's Son!" (Mark 15:39). It seems Mark is making a point here, that it is in Jesus's death where we see him for who he truly is. And it is in Jesus's death that the power of God is revealed. While we should certainly seek to emulate the life of Jesus, it is his death that provides the image for our ethic. It is his willingness to die that gives light to the way he lived.

In our Ash Wednesday services, we are told, "Remember you are dust, and to dust you shall return." The ashes on our forehead at this moment are

---

11. As Gorman puts it, "Justification as reconciliation includes both forgiveness of sins (plural; i.e., transgressions: Rom 3:25; 2 Cor 5:19) and liberation from Sin (singular) as a power (Rom 3:24; 5:15–21)" (Gorman, *Inhabiting the Cruciform God*, 56).

placed in the shape of a cross. While we remember death is inescapable, we also remember that God died too—and because of that, death is not the last word. "For if we have been united with him in a death like his, we will certainly be united with him in a resurrection like his" (Rom 6:5).

9

Resurrecting

GOD DIED. THAT IS a beautiful truth. Yet it becomes beautiful in reverse, the resurrection making it so. Without the resurrection, the cross is a defeat, a catastrophe; it is the end of a movement, of a life. Without the resurrection, the crucifixion would spell the success of oppressive religiopolitical forces. *With the resurrection*, the death of Jesus becomes a *eu*catastrophe; it becomes all we have discussed—a beautiful picture of God's co-suffering, self-emptying power. A power that, through death, has displayed its value for life. Kelly Brown Douglas put it this way, "The resurrection is God's definitive response to the crucifixion itself. It clarifies the essential character of God's power—it is power that values human life." The resurrection, in effect, asserts the "wrongness" of the crucifixion.[1] "Hence, the theological meaning of the crucifixion is not found in the cross alone, that is, through the death of Jesus. Rather the meaning of the crucifixion is found in conjunction with the resurrection—thus it is found in Jesus' very life."[2] In the words of Paul Fiddes, "the risen Christ is the crucified Jesus. Their encounter with the risen Lord compelled the early disciples to look again at the meaning of the cross, and to find a surprising act of God in what seemed to be failure. On the other hand, the atoning work of God in the cross looks forward to resurrection for its completion; the submission of God to death is followed by his conquest of it."[3] One cannot see Jesus for who he truly is without the whole picture. Each phase of Jesus's story inseparably connects to the next. His preexistence, his life, his death, his resurrection, and his

1. Douglas, *What's Faith Got*, 98.
2. Douglas, *What's Faith Got*, 98–99.
3. Fiddes, *Past Event*, 41.

ascension all flow to and from each other. So then, having covered the life and death of Jesus, let us now take a look at what his resurrection tells us.

"Where, O Death, Is Your Sting?"

First Corinthians 15 is a seminal passage on the resurrection, where Paul argues that the Christian faith hinges on Jesus rising from the dead. He writes, "If Christ has not been raised, your faith is futile and you are still in your sins" (1 Cor 15:17). Fortunately, Jesus did rise—and in that, death itself was defeated:

> Death has been swallowed up in victory.
> Where, O death, is your victory?
> Where, O death, is your sting? (1 Cor 15:54–55)

This defeat of death is essential for understanding the importance of the resurrection. Jesus's resurrection, while singular, was done once for all. It is an event that reverberates through all of creation. It was not just a reversal of *his* death but a defeat of the very power of death. What does it mean, then, for the power of death to be defeated? It means (at minimum) the defeat of the fear of death, as well as the defeat of sin. In light of the victory of resurrection, these two realities need to bind us no longer.

Fear of Death

In writing about this victory, the author of Hebrews includes Christ's freeing "those who all their lives were held in slavery by the fear of death" (Heb 2:15). While most people do not live with chronic fear of dying, the fear of death controls us in a myriad of ways, whether by limiting our generosity or prioritizing our safety over the needs of others. In addition, political leaders often use fear of death or danger to stoke fear of the other, and it is quite difficult to love a stranger you have been manipulated to fear. These all run directly counter to the way of Christ—of love for neighbor. Christ's defeat of death provides an antidote to this poison, freeing us from enslavement to our self-centered fear to care for our neighbor with prodigal love.

This lack of fear is illustrated well in C. S. Lewis's Narnian character Reepicheep. At the end of the story's voyage Reepicheep and friends approach a wave that reaches to the sky. On the other side of the wall of water is "Aslan's country."

At that moment, with a crunch, the boat ran aground. The water was too shallow now for it. "This," said Reepicheep, "is where I go on alone." They did not even try to stop him, for everything now felt as if it had been fated or had happened before. They helped him to lower his little coracle. Then he took off his sword ("I shall need it no more," he said) and flung it far away across the lilied sea. Where it fell it stood upright with the hilt above the surface. Then he bade them good-bye, trying to be sad for their sakes; but he was quivering with happiness.[4]

Aslan's country is mysterious in this story; no one knows for sure what is there. And upon his entering, no one saw Reepicheep again. Yet at the same time, he was confident of his fate, even desirous of entering it. Paul shares this sentiment in his Letter to the Philippians, noting that his desires are conflicted. He wants to stay and work for the good of those around him, but he also yearns to be fully with Christ. Given the hope of life after death, there is a new dimension to its arrival. Death is still very much a grim reality,[5] but that grim reality is now tainted with hope. George MacDonald, a writer Lewis admired, imagined it this way in his novel *Phantastes*:

My soul was like a summer evening, after a heavy fall of rain, when the drops are yet glistening on the trees in the last rays of the down-going sun, and the wind of the twilight has begun to blow. The hot fever of life had gone by, and I breathed the clear mountain-air of the land of Death.[6]

In our imaginations we tend to think of death as dark and terrifying, or simply nothing. Certainly not raindrops glistening in trees and clear mountain air. Yet Lewis and MacDonald give us a different picture. Death, to them, is not the storm but the calm that comes after. It can bring beauty and can be entered into with glee, somewhat sad for the people left behind. By defeating death, Jesus ensures that our ends are not the end. We can now live without fear—of death, of failure, even of sin.

4. Lewis, *Voyage of Dawn Treader*, 266.

5. Jesus knew he would raise Lazarus, but he still wept for his friend's death (John 11:35).

6. MacDonald, *Phantastes*, 180.

Defeat of Sin

The power of death manifesting in sin is made clear in the line from Paul following his taunt of death, where he notes that "the sting of death is sin." So in writing "Where, O death, is your sting?," Paul is proclaiming that the power of sin no longer holds one who has found their victory through Christ. This connection between sin and death is not an arbitrary one. In the biblical vision, sin leads to death, not in a rules-oriented punishment sort of way but as a natural progression of consequences. Sin is missing the mark of humanity's vocation of being co-creators with God.[7] As image-bearers, humans were created to create alongside God, to fill the earth and subdue it—or rule over it with care and fertility. Sin becomes our master and disorients us, corrupting that co-creative work, leading us toward destructive ends, for ourselves and the rest of creation. In entering into our humanity, God wraps us up in himself, sin and all. "Christ stands in the dark place where the road taken runs into death, and there sin is 'killed.'"[8] So as we die with him, our sin is destroyed, nailed to the cross (Col 2:14). As we die with Christ, we are then subject to the resurrection of Christ—so we "too might walk in newness of life" (Rom 6:4b). This cancerous power, which has poisoned our lives and our communities, no longer has its hold on us. We are a new creation (2 Cor 5:17). Paul Tillich speaks of sin as a "turning away from the infinite ground of our being."[9] Through this death and resurrection, we are given the opportunity to relinquish our slavery to sin in order to turn back to this "infinite ground." We are given the opportunity be re-created into the kind of beings we were meant to be—a creation enmeshed in the life of God.

This is what forgiveness looks like. God does not simply declare we are forgiven, as if that would be enough. Reconciliation requires a painful journey for both the offender and the offended. As the offended, God sympathetically enters into our experience and he takes on the sin, feeling the weight of the harm done to him. In his death, he extends that arm of forgiveness. We must then make the painful journey of repentance, recognizing our failure and need for reconciliation. In other words, we must die to ourselves. When we join him in that reconciliatory death, we are re-created with him in new life.

---

7. Wright, *Day the Revolution Began*, 86–87.

8. Fiddes, "Salvation," 188.

9. Fiddes, *Past Event*, 12.

There are many hurdles to reconciliation. One is the failure to recognize the harm done; another is the failure to recognize the forgiveness offered. The former, while not always easy, is rather clear cut—in order to be forgiven we must first admit we have done wrong. The latter can often be more subtle. One's reluctance to accept forgiveness can feel like a humble gesture, a way to acknowledge the seriousness of the offense. It can also come from a sense of unworthiness—that one has committed an offense too grievous to be brought back into relationship. Yet if forgiveness has been offered and true repentance has occurred, this reaction is unnecessary and merely prolongs the reconciliation process. The offender must brush off this false humility and accept the truth presented by the offended—that they are forgiven, and reconciliation is possible. For some, though, that is harder than it may first appear, as the existential weight of unworthiness can prove debilitating. Fortunately, even that weight is not one we have to bear alone. Christ, the ultimate Reconciler, works with us in each step of the process. He not only (through his death) offers forgiveness for what we have done wrong but also (through his resurrection) offers a new life in his comforting presence, reminding us of our immeasurable value. Paul writes in Romans, "There is therefore now no condemnation for those in Christ Jesus" (Rom 8:1). As participants in the death of Christ, our sin is condemned, not us. Therefore, this death to ourselves includes death to our shame. We can move on toward our new life in Christ knowing that we are forgiven.

New Creation

Resurrection is not revivification. Jesus did not merely extend his lifespan; he was re-created. As participants in that resurrection, the life given to us is not more of the same. Rather, as Paul put it, "So if anyone is in Christ, there is a new creation: everything old has passed away; see, everything has become new!" (2 Cor 5:17). This new creation, though, comes in stages. According to Paul's Jewish apocalyptic belief, there are two overarching ages to world history. There is the age we are in now, which includes sin, death, and those things that they bring. Then there is the age of God's reign, where God will vindicate himself, and justice and life will prevail. In his Letters to the Corinthians, Paul is arguing that Jesus interrupts our current age, bringing the effects of the coming age into this one. The fabric of the future age is being stretched, overlapping with our own. In this new, overlapping age we still see the effects of the age of death, but with a new hue of hope.

We can experience right now the new life we have in Christ, but it is not yet completed. There is more to come, where all will be set right, where we, and all of creation, will be made whole. Paul writes that we "groan" under the burden of our predicament, but eventually, that which is mortal will be "swallowed up by life" (2 Cor 5:4).

C. S. Lewis calls the incarnation the "Grand Miracle," and it is this miracle on which the whole plot of the world turns. Through his coming (and all that came after), Christ shifts the narrative, and he is bringing all creation with him. "Christ has risen, and so we shall rise."[10] Paul argues that in Christ's resurrection, we see the "first fruits" of what is to come. Borrowing this metaphor, Lewis writes this of the "cosmic summer which is presently coming on":

> St. Peter for a few seconds walked on the water, and the day will come when there will be a re-made universe, infinitely obedient to the will of glorified and obedient men, when we can do all things, when we shall be those gods that we are described as being in Scripture. To be sure, it feels wintry enough still: but often in the very early spring it feels like that. Two thousand years are only a day or two by this scale. A man really ought to say, "The Resurrection happened two thousand years ago" in the same spirit in which he says, "I saw a crocus yesterday." Because we know what is coming behind the crocus. The spring comes slowly down this way; but the great thing is that the corner has been turned. There is, of course, this difference, that in the natural spring the crocus cannot choose whether it will respond or not. We can. We have the power either of withstanding, or of going on into those "high midsummer pomps" in which our Leader, the Son of Man, already dwells, and to which He is calling us. It remains with us to follow or not, to die in this winter, or to go on into that spring and that summer.[11]

We, and the universe along with us, will be remade in the likeness of the resurrected Christ. Our job now is to live into that new creation, forming ourselves to be more like Christ, while at the same time working to bring our world into alignment with that soon-to-be re-created world. This, in the end, is what it looks like to be a part of the kingdom of God, and it is why we pray "Your kingdom come. Your will be done, on earth as it is in heaven" (Matt 6:10). As Moltmann put it, "The gospel is the invitation

10. Lewis, Grand Miracle, 62.
11. Lewis, Grand Miracle, 62.

to God's future. People who believe the gospel experience the powers of the future world (Heb. 6:5). They move into the springtime of the new creation."[12] There is a metaphysical consistency in this connection between God's reconciling act and the bringing of life. If sin brings death, then being one with God should naturally bring life. The great church father Athanasius made this connection in the fourth century, writing, "There is thus no inconsistency between creation and salvation; for the One Father has employed the same Agent for both works, effecting the salvation of the world through the same Word who made it in the beginning."[13] The preincarnate Christ—who John noted was there in the beginning, bringing all things into being—is the same one crucified for our sake and resurrected to bring us new life. He is the source of life itself. To be in Christ is to be made new, and to participate in his work is to bring that new life to everything, and every person, we encounter, doing the same work he did in his life—healing, teaching, welcoming the outcast, lifting up the oppressed.

Resurrection Life

Paul's teaching in 1 Cor 15, that Christ rose from the dead, is presented in order to correct some Corinthian misconceptions. The Corinthians had come to separate the body and the spirit—believing that Jesus saved their souls, so what they did with their bodies did not matter. It is tempting to view salvation in this lens, and it can materialize in various ways. One way is in the fashion of the Corinthians; in denying the value of embodied life, they threw off restraint and embraced hedonism. Another method is one more common to modern American Christianity, caring only for the salvation of "souls" and not for the material lives they live. To this point, Martin Luther King Jr. wrote, "A religion that professes a concern for the souls of men and is not equally concerned about the slums that damn them, the economic conditions that strangle them, and the social conditions that cripple them, is a spiritually moribund religion."[14] In affirming the resurrection, Paul is affirming the body and what we do with it, which should include care for the bodies of others. "To proclaim the resurrection of Christ is to declare God's triumph over death and therefore the meaningfulness of embodied

---

12. Moltmann, *Jesus Christ for Today's World*, 146.

13. Athanasius, *On the Incarnation*, 26.

14. King., *Strength to Love*, 160–61.

life."[15] Or to borrow again from Moltmann, "Resurrection is not a consoling opium, soothing us with the promise of a better world in the hereafter. It is the energy for a rebirth of this life. The hope doesn't point to another world. It is focused on the redemption of this one."[16] In our celebration of the resurrection we tend toward the saccharine, but the first Easter was anything but. It was an earth-shattering revolution reverberating through our corporeal world. Living out the truth of the resurrection means living wholly embodied in the present, experiencing the depth of what it means to be a human made from the dust in the image of God, participating in the redemption God has started and will eventually complete.

The Christian life, therefore, is not one lived in mere hope for future resurrection. The Christian life is one engaged in the daily act of resurrecting. The resurrection is not a closed fact, but a way of life.[17] We die to ourselves while bringing life to everything and everyone around us. We are reconciled; therefore we reconcile (2 Cor. 5:18).

An Exact Imprint

The writer of Hebrews tells us that Jesus is "the reflection of God's glory and the exact imprint of God's very being" (Heb 1:3). If Jesus is who he said he was, then God is a God of resurrecting. This then means that our longing for life after death, our hope that there is something more to this life, is all true. Our hope for the afterlife, then, is not mere sentimentality; it is a grounded and eternal hope. Maybe we hate death so much because we all intuitively know that it is not the way things are meant to be. Maybe it feels wrong because it is wrong. The story of Jesus shows us that God values life, he values us, our very beings, and he won't leave us in our pain. He will always and forever be lifting us up, continually drawing us in to his loving, life-giving embrace. This is what it means for Jesus to be the Thesis.

15. Hays, *First Corinthians*, 278, 253.

16. Moltmann, *Jesus Christ for Today's World*, 81.

17. Moltmann, *Jesus Christ for Today's World*, 81.

Part 4

Applying the Thesis

To be a Christian does not mean that we are to change the world, but rather that we must live as witnesses to the world that God has changed. We should not be surprised, therefore, if the way we live makes the change visible.

—STANLEY HAUERWAS, *MATTHEW*[1]

The World God Has Changed

IN CHRIST, GOD SETS the world right. He defeats death and brings life. This is a reality already, but not yet, accomplished. In the meantime, we get to participate in this reality. We get to enter into the story where Jesus is the Thesis, by making him the Thesis of our own lives. This is a life of love, of hope, of justice. A life that demands our all but returns an infinite and eternal life.

1. Hauerwas, *Matthew*, 25.

10

A Christocentric Ethic

IN 2 CORINTHIANS, AFTER declaring our status as new creation, Paul writes: "All this is from God, who reconciled us to himself through Christ, and has given us the ministry of reconciliation" (2 Cor 5:18). In his mind, our reconciliation with God necessitates reconciliation with others.[1] Michael Gorman finds this correlation in another of Paul's letters, noting that in Rom 1:18, "Paul refers to the two basic categories of sin as *asebeia* and *adikia*, impiety and injustice, sins against God and sins against fellow humans."[2] The solution, the death and resurrection of Christ, should then produce in us a reversal of those two kinds of sin. "In other words, there can be no justification without transformation. The justified are those who have begun the process of replacing *asebeia* and *adikia* with *pistis* [faith] and *dikaiosyne/agape* [justice/love] by the power of the Spirit."[3] In replacing impiety with faith we recognize Christ as our King. In replacing injustice with justice and love, we submit ourselves to his work in the world. One directly flows to the other. "Christ isn't merely a person. He is a road too. And the person who believes him takes the same road he took. There is no christology without christopraxis, no knowledge of Christ without the practice of Christ."[4] We must ask ourselves, then, how do we live out this

1. Chris Green puts it this way: "We have to acknowledge that the *call* to follow Christ is indistinguishable from the *calling* to share in his life and to work his works. Or, to put it yet another way, our salvation does not happen apart from our being taken up into collaborative participation with God's work of reconciling the world to himself" (Green, *Sanctifying Interpretation*, 15).

2. Gorman, *Inhabiting the Cruciform God*, 50.

3. Gorman, *Inhabiting the Cruciform God*, 51.

4. Moltmann, *Jesus Christ for Today's World*, 47.

practice of Christ? Put differently, what would an ethic look like with Jesus as its Thesis?

Bonhoeffer and the Form of Christ

At the heart of ethics is the question, what is right and wrong? Right and wrong, though, are realities dependent on the nature of ourselves and the world. One can only know if a use of something is "right" if they know what the purpose of that thing is. Dietrich Bonhoeffer, the renowned German theologian and ethicist, began his book on ethics by making this foundational point. Writing from a prison cell, captured (and later executed) by the Nazi regime, he argued that:

> Those who wish even to focus on the problem of a Christian ethic are faced with an outrageous demand—from the outset they must give up, as inappropriate to this topic, the very two questions that led them to deal with the ethical problem: "How can I be good?" and "How can I accomplish something good?" Instead they must ask the wholly other, completely different question: what is the will of God? This demand is radical precisely because it presupposes a decision about ultimate reality, that is, a decision of faith. When the ethical problem presents itself essentially as the question of my own being good and doing good, the decision has already been made that the self and the world are the ultimate realities. All ethical reflection then has the goal that I be good, and that the world—by my action—becomes good. If it turns out, however, that these realities, myself and the world, are themselves embedded in a wholly other ultimate reality, namely, the reality of God the Creator, Reconciler, and Redeemer, then the ethical problem takes on a whole new aspect. Of ultimate importance, then, is not that I become good, or that the condition of the world be improved by my efforts, but that the reality of God show itself everywhere to be the ultimate reality.[5]

According to Bonhoeffer, the question of right and wrong, of how I should live in the world, is subsumed under the ultimate reality of God himself. God is the Creator of our universe, the only infinite being, utterly independent of any other. Our selves and our world, on the other hand, depend on God for our existence. If we desire to know what is right, we must first seek to understand who God is and what he wills for our lives.

5. Bonhoeffer, *Ethics*, 1.

Bonhoeffer continues, "Since God, however, as ultimate reality is no other than the self-announcing, self-witnessing, self-revealing God in Jesus Christ, the question of good can only find its answer in Christ."[6] Jesus Christ is the "exact imprint of God's very being" (Heb 1:3); he is the one through whom all things came into existence (John 1:3); and he revealed himself through his life, death, and resurrection. If we want to know what it means to live ethically, we look to him, because he is where we see the will of God perfectly embodied.[7] Therefore, the Christian ethic is not one based on principles, or rules to abide by, but a person we intend to reflect, desiring that his reality be made real in our lives and our world. Put differently, we are to work as Jesus taught us to pray, "Your kingdom come, your will be done, on earth as it is in heaven" (Matt 6:10).

This reality has far-reaching implications for how we think about ethical living. While we may desire to depend on concrete rules to regulate our behavior, an ethic founded on a person eschews that kind of orderliness. It recognizes the embodied and contextual nature of our decisions and seeks to mold us into a certain type of person. That is not to say the Christian ethic is relative, for as Bonhoeffer writes, "The form of Christ is one and the same at all times and in all places."[8] Yet, it is important to note, "God did not become an idea, a principle, a program, a universally valid belief, or a law; God became human. That means that the form of Christ, though it certainly is and remains one and the same, intends to take form in real human beings, and thus in quite different ways."[9] We see here in Bonhoeffer's formulation two important truths. The first is that God as ultimate reality makes demands on our moral lives. We do not have the authority to decide what is right and wrong; rather, we must look to Christ to discover how to live. And second, that "way to live" is concrete and human. It is not an abstract ethic detached from lived reality but attempts to get at how Christ may take form in our particular moment and context.[10]

The concrete and human nature of an ethic founded on Christ is essential for how we engage our theorizing about ethics. It should motivate us

---

6. Bonhoeffer, *Ethics*, 2.

7. It is important to note here that this does not mean that a person who is not a follower of Jesus cannot be ethical. It simply means that, when someone is acting ethically, they are acting like Christ.

8. Bonhoeffer, *Ethics*, 44.

9. Bonhoeffer, *Ethics*, 44.

10. Bonhoeffer, *Ethics*, 45.

to avoid getting lost in theory and look more closely at the lived reality of the topics we are discussing. A common unfortunate by-product of thinking deeply about ethics is that one might forget that the theory is not the point; the people are. We can get caught up in arguments about whether something is right or wrong, forgetting that the decision is taking place in a messy world of uncertainty regarding the lives of very real and vulnerable people. The kenotic nature of Christ pushes us to continually consider how the theory is embodied.

Bonhoeffer also speaks to the complexity of this application, emphasizing that ethical judgments are made "in the middle," where our criterion for good is often not directly applicable to the situation at hand. In our fallen world, we rarely encounter good and evil in "pure" forms, where some ethical theory can clearly guide us to the right decision. In these moments, we must rely on wisdom, using moral judgment to discern not the "absolute good act" but "the next step in a path of obedience, a path whose end is clear while the middle distance is not. Only in this way is Christian ethics a journey of faith and hope, and not of sight."[11]

In these moments, it is certainly helpful to look at principles we have discovered through our engagement with Christ, Scripture, church tradition, and elsewhere. To say that principles are not the basis of our ethic is not to say they are wholly invalid.[12] In fact, in chapter 3, we argued that the moral principles to which cultures throughout time have appealed find their ultimate reality in Christ himself. These principles, then, can be a tool[13] to help us in our larger goal of being formed to the image of Christ, working toward the eventual resurrection, where all things will be made new.[14] Our decisions in these middle moments should always have this end in mind and should always bring us a little closer to it.

11. Brock, *Singing Ethos of God*, 90.

12. McCabe, *Law, Love and Language*, 22.

13. Principle-based ethical theory is referred to as deontology. Others, like consequentialism (theory prioritizing the consequences of an action) and virtue ethics (theory prioritizing virtues) can also be valuable tools in ethical decision-making.

14. Catholic theologian and philosopher Herbert McCabe put this helpfully, writing, "I have not, in this book, tried to apply Christian principles to particular moral questions because it seems to me that Christianity does not in the first place propose a set of moral principles. As I suggested in my first chapter, I do not think that such principles are out of place in Christianity; without them the notion of love may collapse into vagueness and unmeaning, but Christianity is essentially about our communication with each other in Christ, our participation in the world of the future" (McCabe, *Law, Love and Language*, 172).

The Beginning of Wisdom

Wisdom is an essential component of the Christ-centered ethic. Lives lived "in the middle," where problems are messy and solutions all but obvious, require the development of discernment. This is one theme we find throughout the wisdom literature of the Hebrew Bible and the New Testament that follows it. Even the more simplistic works on wisdom, like Proverbs, still assume that one must work to develop it. And according to Proverbs, that development starts with "the fear of the Lord" (Prov 1:7). Old Testament scholar Ronald E. Clements notes that this phrase, "the fear of the Lord," "implies not anxiety and dread but unwavering devotion to the God of Israel."[15]

This fits together beautifully with our discussion in chapter 7, where Jesus is Wisdom made human, as well as the King heralding the kingdom of heaven. The development of wisdom is important because our King is Wisdom. And our unwavering devotion to (or fear of) him is the beginning of wisdom in us. If ethics should start with a commitment to the will of God, the ultimate reality, and Jesus is the exact imprint of that God, then, of course, a wholehearted commitment to follow after him will develop our ability to discern right from wrong.

Scripture and Ethics

The New Testament contains a multiplicity of ethical teaching. However, New Testament scholar Richard Hays argues that there is a unity in that multiplicity. It is not the unity of a dogmatic system but a "looser unity of a collection of documents that, in various ways, retell and comment upon a single fundamental story." The story is, in his words, as follows:

> The God of Israel, the creator of the world, has acted (astoundingly) to rescue a lost and broken world through the death and resurrection of Jesus; the full scope of that rescue is not yet apparent, but God has created a community of witnesses to this good news, the church. While awaiting the grand conclusion of the story, the church, empowered by the Holy Spirit, is called to reenact the loving obedience of Jesus Christ and thus to serve as a sign of God's redemptive purposes for the world.[16]

15. Clements, "Proverbs."
16. Hays, *Moral Vision*, 193.

The Christian ethic is to "reenact the loving obedience of Jesus." We are to reprise in our own contexts the song he has already played—the song we have outlined in the previous three chapters. We are to be his disciples, just like the first, walking alongside him, students of his life and teaching. To be a follower of Christ means not simply regarding him as a good teacher or a hero who saved the world; following Christ is not a mere change of attitude or perspective. It entails a new way of life, worked out in concrete ways, for the benefit of the sick, the poor, and the oppressed. In following Jesus we are surrendering our lives; we are dying to ourselves. Through that death then comes new life.

Hays's perspective reveals the importance of Scripture in our Christocentric ethic. Through reading Scripture, we encounter the story of Christ we are meant to reenact. In the Old Testament, we see the ways God worked through a chosen people to bring about redemption in the world; in the Gospels, we see Jesus Christ himself, the fullest revelation of that God of Israel; and in the rest of the New Testament, we see the church working out what it means to live in the world as followers of that God. What we find in Acts and the letters of the New Testament is, as Hays points out, not a dogmatic system—the incarnating God rarely works that way—but rather God-inspired followers of Jesus working to apply the story of Jesus to the life of the church. It is then not through a systematic collection of biblical commands where we find our ethic, but rather through an encounter with God himself in the pages of Scripture. We are to do as the New Testament writers have done before us. They experienced the risen Jesus, then attempted to apply what they experienced to their particular situations.

This approach to the ethics of Scripture means treating it not as a mere resource for life advice but as a place of meditation.[17] It is through a life of meditating on Scripture that we discover God's will for our lives. On this point, Bonhoeffer writes, "God's Word is not a collection of eternally valid principles that we can have at our disposal at any time we wish. It is the Word of God that is new every day for us in the endless riches of its interpretation. Meditation (that is, prayerful consideration of Scripture) and interpretation are both essential to anyone who seeks God's commandments and not just her own thoughts."[18] Through these acts of meditation and interpretation we encounter God and his will, then work to apply it.

17. For more on the relationship between Scripture and ethics, see Brock, *Singing Ethos of God*.

18. Bonhoeffer, *Meditating on the Word*, 122.

This requires a delight in the word of God, like the psalmist who writes, "I treasure your word in my heart, so that I may not sin against you" (Ps 119:11). In detailing Bonhoeffer's approach to Scripture and ethics, Brian Brock notes:

> God's Word is thus not an ethical program but a heuristic, and a negative heuristic at that: it strips away our divergent self-ref-erential hermeneutics to reveal our total dependence on God's presence, and so to direct us to his real (as opposed to imagined) presence. That is why a catalog approach to the moral passages of Scripture is doomed to failure: only when Scripture is "treasured in the heart" in all its bewildering complexity will its true unity in Christ begin to emerge. This unity, again, cannot be in the first instance conceptual, though it will have conceptual content; it will be in Christ and in his meeting us in the course of making us real humans as we take real steps of faith in our historical context.[19]

Our mission as humans is to be the image of God in the world, medi-ating his rule. When we begin to internalize this role, the aforementioned approach to Scripture makes more sense. In essence, we are created to in-terpret.[20] Our approach to Scripture is in step with our approach to life in general. We meditate on God, submitting ourselves to the rule of Christ our King, and we participate in his story, interpreting God's will and embody-ing it as we reconcile the world alongside him.

God at Work

The story of Jesus compels us to love, to care for the sick, the poor, and the oppressed. It teaches us that injustice does not have to be the norm. Rather, we can and should work toward the eventual future of a redeemed creation. When one develops this compassion, though, it is quite easy to despair at the near-infinite complexity of modern life and the seeming impossibility of progress. Much of the change that needs to happen in our world must occur at the societal level. If we are going to solve problems like global hun-ger or racial injustice, we need large swaths of our society to get on board. We, as individuals, do not have the power to "change the world." If we are responsible for saving the world, it will never happen.

---

19. Brock, *Singing Ethos of God*, 85.
20. Green, *Sanctifying Interpretation*, 41.

The despair only increases when we consider our own moral lives. While we tend to look outward to name the ills of our world, a moment's introspection will reveal we have work within ourselves that must be done, and it is not always easy to do it. We long to become "better people" yet often find ourselves lacking. Time and time again we try to be better, and time and time again we fail. If we are responsible for saving ourselves, it will never happen.

The beauty of the Christian ethic is that we are not alone. God will save the world, whether we want him to or not. By his grace, we have the opportunity to engage in that world-saving work—and because the end does not depend on us, we can engage in it without worry. We can work toward the redemption of the world with a hopeful determination. Knowing that our work matters for the individuals we care for yet, at the same time, the world will be made right no matter what.

The same goes for our own moral formation. At the conclusion of the Christ hymn in Phil 2, Paul encourages his audience to work out their own salvation "with fear and trembling; for it is God who is at work in you, enabling you both to will and to work for his good pleasure" (Phil 2:12b–13). Our formation is deeply important work. It should absolutely be done in "fear and trembling." In humility, we must acknowledge our own lack of wisdom and failure to live up to the goodness of God. We must submit ourselves to the kingship of Christ, recognizing that he knows better than we do. But in submitting, we recognize that we are not alone in that work. God is at work in us through the Holy Spirit, enabling us to become more like him. Earlier in Philippians, Paul writes, "I am sure of this, that he who started a good work in you will carry it on to completion until the day of Christ Jesus" (1:6 CSB). A Christocentric ethic is not meant to be a shame-filled grind where we will ourselves up a mountain, punishing ourselves for every wrong step. Rather, it is taking the hand of Christ as he leads us in a graceful dance. Adjusting as we misstep, he pulls us back in to his loving embrace.

11

A Christocentric Sexual Ethic

WE NEED A NEW SEXUAL ETHIC. The one we have adopted in many of our churches has not led to the flourishing of our youth but to needless guilt and shame. The one we have adopted in our society, while aimed toward liberation, has left countless trapped in empty hookup after hookup, unable to attain a life in meaningful relationship. And in both spheres, we find rampant sexual abuse, often swept under the rug.[1] A new way of thinking and living in the realm of sexuality is necessary, new boundaries must be drawn. While talk of boundaries may, at first, appear stifling—even repressive—it is important to remember that everyone believes there should be guardrails to sex. "Sex-positivity" may be the mantra of our day, but even the sex-positive want limitations. The problem is where to place them. And further, how they are ethically grounded. Is consent enough of a guide? Maybe some ethic of love? Or might there be more to a good ethic of sex— like justice, mercy, or generosity?

Part of our problem today is sex's taboo nature. Church people rarely want to talk about it—and when they do, it's nearly always reserved for the youth, warning of the dangers in premarital sex and foretelling the bliss awaiting them in the marriage bed. As much as talk of sex is taboo

---

1. The #MeToo movement has brought much of this to the surface in the broader culture. Regarding the church, cases in recent news include a report on the Southern Baptist Convention, including accounts of over seven hundred pastors that convention leaders kept secret (Shellnut, "Southern Baptists Refused"); Kanakuk Kamps, a Branson-based church camp with decades of unreported sexual abuse (French, "Survivors, Ex-employees"); and Ravi Zacharias, a Christian apologist who "leveraged his reputation. . . to abuse massage therapists. . . over more than a decade" (Silliman and Shellnut, "Ravi Zacharias Hid"). As this footnote is already depressingly long, I will end it here.

in churches, so it is in popular culture as well. This taboo, though, is in sex's potential limitations. To speak of limiting sexual activity beyond the bounds of consent brings accusations of repressiveness or, in some cases, "kink-shaming." Ethicist Margaret Farley argues that "despite our contemporary openness in displaying and deploying sex, we carry too much baggage regarding sex into our moral discernment and judgments. . . . Thus, a necessary step in the formulation of a contemporary sexual ethic must be to move sexuality more completely from the realm of the pre-ethical (the realm of taboos) to the ethical."[2] In order to develop an approach to sexuality that takes seriously its pleasure, its danger, and its ubiquity in our lives, moving past taboo is necessary. As embodied creatures, sex is part of our lives, and always will be. We must take it seriously, speak about it more openly, and refuse to shy away from its constantly arising quandaries.

As a society, we must grapple with the limitations of a freedom-focused, consent-only ethic and the ways it is failing us all. And as Christians, we can no longer hold on to our shallow, taboo-driven ethic. We need something deeper, more wholistic, and more true. This chapter is an attempt to provide the beginnings of that. While we do not address every question (we never could), it is, we propose, a helpful foundation for thinking more deeply about sexuality as followers of Jesus.[3] Jesus is, as we have already discussed, our foundation for ethical thinking. While it may seem odd to say that our celibate Savior should be the Thesis of our sexual ethic, it is true. His way, in the end, will produce a more just and loving sexuality. In order to unpack that, it may be helpful to start with some teaching of his own.

The Power of Sexual Desire

The Sermon on the Mount is, in many ways, Jesus's manifesto on ethics. In it, he describes the kind of kingdom he is bringing and what it looks like to participate in that kingdom. He begins with the description, offering blessings to many, including those who are poor in spirit, who mourn, who thirst for righteousness (or justice), and who are merciful. In this, we see the way of Jesus as one that brings about hope for the poor and the oppressed, one that pursues justice through the means of mercy. Following

2. Farley, *Just Love*, 177–78.

3. While we do not explicitly address polyamory, lesbian and gay relationships, or any number of other important topics, we think this chapter serves as a useful foundation for which further thought on those issues can be grounded.

this, he tells his disciples they are the salt and light of the world—people who, through their good works, will reveal the glory of God to others. He then offers his own teaching on some commands from the Hebrew Bible. Starting with anger, then moving on to adultery, divorce, oaths, and retaliation, he presents an ethic motivated by love, with a realism that accounts for our human susceptibility to be enslaved by our desires.

Concerning anger, he says, "You have heard that it was said to those of ancient times, 'You shall not murder'; and 'whoever murders shall be liable to judgment.' But I say to you that if you are angry with a brother or sister, you will be liable to judgment" (Matt 5:21–22a). Concerning adultery, he says similarly, "You have heard that it was said, 'You shall not commit adultery.' But I say to you that everyone who looks at a woman with lust has already committed adultery with her in his heart" (Matt 5:27–28). In each of these, he shifts our focus. "These shifts are important," writes New Testament scholar William Loader, "because they also reflect a shift from what can be prosecuted in a court of law, murder and adultery, to how we relate to one another, where attitudes matter, not just actions."[4] Here Jesus urges us to think more deeply than mere legality when it comes to right and wrong. Our attitudes toward others matter, not just our behavior. While murder is certainly a dehumanizing act, as it extinguishes the life from another, hatred is a form of dehumanization as well—one that fails to recognize the other as the beloved, image-bearing child of God they are. Our sexual attitudes toward others matter, then, as well. Lust in this context is not the mere recognition of another's sexual appeal. It is taking that recognition, then adding fuel to that desire for them. It is using the image of another for your own pleasure. Our terminology today is *objectification*, which fits well. As hatred dehumanizes, so does lust, reducing a person to mere object for our own gratification. Jesus urges us to avoid both dehumanizing anger and dehumanizing sexual desire.

One assumption in Jesus's argument here is the power of these attitudes to produce behavior. Hatred, it seems, is a significant motivator. If we want to refrain from committing acts of violence, it makes sense to keep our feelings of anger in check; same with sexual desire. Personally and socially, sexual desire is a potent force. Song of Songs gives us an apt image for this desire in its description of love. It says, "For love is strong as death, passion fierce as the grave. Its flashes are flashes of fire, a raging flame. Many waters cannot quench love, neither can floods drown it. If one

4. Loader, *Sexuality in New Testament*, 66–67.

offered for love all the wealth of one's house, it would be utterly scorned" (Song 8:6b–7). Desire is a raging flame, one that must be directed to be beneficial; unchecked flame will eventually bring destruction. This all-consuming nature of sexual desire is part of its appeal. We become enraptured by the experience. It captivates us, bringing our attention solely to the other person, relieving us of our anxieties and doubts. Yet when that desire fails to properly account for its object, it can cease to be loving. Margaret Farley puts it this way: "Desire for another may outrun our love for another, so that our love becomes love primarily for ourselves. All of this means that desire, too, can have norms; and the norms, not surprisingly, have a lot to do with the concrete reality of what is loved."[5] This is where we begin to clearly see our Christocentric ethic's application to sexuality. If we are to be formed to the image of Christ—and Christ is the kenotic King, the one who constantly gives himself up for the other in love—then we must, even in our sexuality, operate in that self-giving love. When our desire fails to account for the concrete reality of the desired—fails to love them as human beings made in the image of God—it ceases to be ethical.

This is why Jesus urges us not to lust. It is not self-giving love but self-gratifying desire. Lust sees the other as an object for our own pleasure, rather than a person to be loved. There is a difference, then, between the healthy sexual desire one feels for their spouse and the lust one directs toward a stranger. The former is one of mutuality, where the desire is interspersed with a life of care; the latter is mere self-gratification. The experience of the person on the receiving end of those experiences can often intuit the difference. The former experiences acceptance, even belovedness. The latter often feels used, resulting in disgust. While these are both experiences of sexual desire, they are far from the same. Jesus is by no means claiming that sexual desire is inherently wrong. It becomes wrong when it fails to see the desired as a whole person made in the image of God—worthy of dignity, respect, and love. And this happens when we fail to properly direct our affections, when we fuel them wantonly. In other words: when we lust.

It seems rather obvious to note the power of sexual desire, yet our ethical frameworks for sexuality rarely take this into account. A Christocentric ethic is an immensely grounded one. It seeks to account for reality—the reality of the desired and their image-bearing essence, as well as the reality of sexual desire and its roaring flame-like nature. The destructiveness of this flame is obvious when reaching its zenith of ill use, in the varieties of

5. Farley, *Just Love*, 206.

sexual abuse with which we are all too familiar. Its subtle destructiveness comes in the dehumanizing stares, the catcalls, and the sinking glances. Each of these is a failure to account for the realities of being human.

Marriage and Discipleship

Mark 10 reveals a little more about Jesus's take on sexuality, in the context of a teaching on divorce. Some Pharisees come and ask him, "Is it lawful for a man to divorce his wife?" (Mark 10:2). Matthew and Mark, in their account of this event, both note the Pharisees were testing Jesus in this question. He was teaching all around the area, claiming to be authoritative, and people were following. So they did what was done for all Jewish teachers: they lobbed him a tough question to test his interpretive skills. It was a contentious issue—and still is, yet for different reasons. Divorce was significantly one-sided, a right reserved for the man who "owned" his wife. Jesus acknowledges this right but continues, "Because of your hardness of heart [Moses] wrote this commandment for you. But from the beginning of creation, 'God made them male and female.' 'For this reason a man shall leave his father and mother and be joined to his wife, and the two shall become one flesh.' So they are no longer two, but one flesh. Therefore what God has joined together, let no one separate" (Mark 10:6–9). This phrase "one flesh" occurs throughout scripture. Here Jesus is quoting its first occurrence, in Gen 2. He not only quotes it but emphasizes it through repetition, an ancient way of adding an exclamation point. He uses this doctrine to make his final point: since in marriage two become one flesh, Jesus argues, a man should not divorce his wife.

Mark then shifts the narrative to the conversation after, where Jesus and his disciples are, it appears, recounting the events of the day. They ask him to elaborate. Jesus says: "Whoever divorces his wife and marries another commits adultery against her; and if she divorces her husband and marries another, she commits adultery" (Mark 10:11–12). There are two important points we should expand on here regarding Jesus's answer. The first is elucidated well by Richard Hays. While this passage may, on the surface, seem ordinary to modern readers, it was an eminently surprising teaching. The greatest surprise, he writes, "is the statement that the man who remarries after divorcing his wife commits adultery *against her*. This declaration posits a fundamental redefinition of adultery; in Jewish Law and tradition, adultery was a property offense, a form of stealing a man's property by 'taking' his wife. Thus, adultery could by definition be committed only against a man, for the husband was not in any reciprocal sense regarded as the sexual property of the wife. Jesus' teaching, however, changes the rules of the game with one bold stroke."[6] Jesus flips the script, putting the man and the woman on equal footing, forcing his listeners to rethink their approach to marriage itself.

The second point to expand on helps us understand the first, which is that this passage in Mark is set within the context of teaching on discipleship. Mark 8:31—10:45 is an extended reflection on what it means to follow Christ and to reflect his way of life. Mark's central image for that way is the cross. It is a *cruciform*, or cross-shaped, way. Again in the words of Hays, "for Mark, discipleship is necessarily cruciform, and marriage is to be understood within the vocation of discipleship."[7] Discipleship is not one feature of being a Christian; it is our way of being, transforming the way we do all things. It is another word for what we have been talking about the last few chapters, our participation in the life of Christ. Marriage is inevitably drawn into that. With this cruciformity as the backdrop, Jesus's teaching becomes clear. In marriage, two become one flesh and are to love each other with a Christlike love, a love where one continually gives themselves up for the other. In bringing both the man and wife to equal footing, Jesus affirms this cruciform way. One cannot love the other while lording over them the threat of divorce, especially when it is a threat the other cannot wield. This mutuality is essential to Jesus's view of marriage and sexuality. To get a more robust picture of this, we should move now to Paul and his teaching on sexuality.

Paul on Sex

The Corinthian Christians were falling prey to some teaching claiming that what they did with their bodies did not ultimately matter. Their souls were saved, so they could act as they wished—in this case, in a sexually promiscuous manner. In 1 Cor 6, Paul quotes what seem to be mantras from the Corinthians and offers responses in quick succession. He quotes them saying "All things are lawful for me" and responds, "But not all things are beneficial." He quotes, "All things are lawful for me," and responds, "But I will not be dominated by anything." And finally, he quotes, "Food is meant for the stomach and the stomach for food, and God will destroy both one

---

6. Hays, *Moral Vision*, 352.

7. Hays, *Moral Vision*, 349.

and the other."[8] Then he responds, "The body is not meant for fornication but for the Lord, and the Lord for the body." In setting up his teaching on sexuality, Paul reflects Jesus's concerns—namely, the concern of mastery. Jesus is our King, so we eschew all others, even the "king" called pleasure, or self-gratification, or appetite. If allowed, these desires will in fact take over our lives. That is what desires do, if left unchecked—they are a hunger never satisfied, only wanting more. This is not a scare tactic, but rather a grim reminder of something we see in people, including ourselves, every day. The good news is we can forgo those masters, the ones who are never satisfied, always and forever demanding more *from* us, and give ourselves to the Master who always and forever gives himself *for* us. Our bodies are meant for the Lord, who is for us.[9]

Committing to not be mastered by pleasure is a path frustratingly counter to our world's trajectory. We are a consumer culture, with ads ever more catered to our particular tastes. It takes work to refrain from that way of life, but it is necessary to do so. Our health—spiritual, mental, and physical—depends on it. In choosing Christ as our King, we find a Master who gives rather than takes, who loves without restraint, who cares for us as human beings. That cannot be said of all the other masters we give ourselves to, including the master "sexual desire."

Paul goes on to write, "Do you not know that your bodies are members of Christ? Should I therefore take the members of Christ and make them members of a prostitute? Never! Do you not know that whoever is united to a prostitute becomes one body with her? For it is said, 'The two shall be one flesh.' But anyone united to the Lord becomes one spirit with him" (1 Cor 6:15–17). He ends this section writing, "Do you not know that your body is a temple of the Holy Spirit within you, which you have from God, and that you are not your own? For you were bought with a price; therefore glorify God in your body" (1 Cor 6:19–20). Paul's point here is not about prostitution, per se. Insert any other casual sexual relationship and his message remains: we should be concerned about what dominates

---

8. The ancient Greek did not use quotation marks, so some work must be done in order for us (not knowing the slogans like the Corinthians) to determine where they should lie. Interpreters disagree on the final one, but this placement seems to be the most reasonable, as the Corinthians were promoting a spiritual reality divested of the body. Gordon Fee argues persuasively for this view in his commentary. See Fee, *First Epistle to Corinthians*, 279–83.

9. This is the foundation for the discipline of fasting. It is a commitment to not be dominated by any pleasure, reminding us of our true Master and King.

us, and as members of Christ, he alone should be our Master. Paul uses some playful wordplay to make this point, noting that we were "bought with a price;"[10] "Christ has bought the Christian. The Christian should not be buying the prostitute." Christ's purchase is not one with money—as if an image-bearing human could be priced in such a way—but with the life of God himself. He is our Master who becomes so by becoming a slave, giving himself for us (Phil 2:7). He is a Master who never dominates nor denigrates but brings abundant life.

As mentioned before, the creation account in Gen 2 is the first occurrence of "one flesh," rooting the concept in the fundamental design of humanity. Jesus then appeals to this fundamental truth when teaching on divorce, claiming that in marriage one flesh is established and should not be separated.[11] The phrase connotes not only the bond of marriage but also of sexual intimacy, and is used throughout Scripture to refer to both. Given adultery as the focal point in Jesus's teaching, it is clear that he has both in mind when using the phrase. Paul continues this usage here, where he claims that when one has sex with a prostitute, they become one flesh with her. Paul argues that something about the act of sex has a permanent effect on the two engaging in it.[12] This fits well with Jesus's teaching that since the two are one flesh, they should not be separated. While Jesus's argument is regarding the tail end of the relationship and Paul the beginning, they both assume that through sexual intercourse two become one in a real and permanent way.

How this works is unclear, as nowhere in Scripture do we get a detailed explanation of the concept of "one flesh." Paul speaks to lack of clarity in his

---

10. Loader, *Sexuality in New Testament*, 73.

11. It should be noted here that the New Testament does offer instances where divorce is acceptable. In Matt 5:32 Jesus gives adultery as grounds for separation. Paul, in 1 Cor 7 repeats Jesus's teaching that divorce should be avoided, while at the same time giving advice to those who experience it nonetheless, including offering freedom for believing women who have been divorced from unbelieving husbands. It is our opinion that divorce should be avoided as much as possible, but as discussed in the previous chapter, the principle itself is not our ultimate guide. We must act in wisdom, with the council of reliable elders, to determine the most Christlike path for our lives. It seems to us that, among adultery, there may be other grounds for divorce not mentioned in the New Testament—most notably, instances of abuse, both physical and verbal. In all these cases, the victim has been subjected to the perpetrator's severing of the "one flesh" through adultery, abuse, etc., and they may acknowledge that already completed severing through the process of divorce.

12. Loader, *Sexuality in New Testament*, 73.

Letter to the Ephesians, where he writes, "For this reason a man will leave his father and mother and be joined to his wife, and the two will become one flesh. This mystery is profound, but I am talking about Christ and the church" (Eph 5:31–32 CSB). It is a mystery, but it is a mystery in a similar way as the relationship between Christ and the church—a mystery we cannot know fully, but we can know assuredly. We are one with Christ, taken into his life. In the same way, the man and woman become one, taken into each other's lives.

What can we conclude about this "one flesh" from its uses mentioned in this chapter? First, it is created in sexual intercourse. Sexual intercourse creates a bond between two people that is not merely physical. This is a truth counter to hookup culture, which wants to say that sex can be stripped from relationship, that it can be engaged in one-night stands without consequence. While this can certainly become true in a sense—with individuals numbing themselves to the wholistic nature of sex to the point where they do not experience its fullest reality—it is not its true nature, and we harm ourselves (and reduce our pleasure) in ignoring it. Sexual intercourse, as Richard Hays put it, "is not merely the satisfaction of individual appetites, as eating is, but it links two persons together—literally and spiritually. It effects what it symbolizes and symbolizes what it effects."[13] To act as if our sexuality can be reduced to mere animalism is to live counter to our humanity. We are not mere animals.

Second, it is permanent. The two become one flesh, and this one flesh persists indefinitely. It is an indissoluble bond. This bond brings us to the third conclusion, that the concept of one flesh is the foundation of marriage.[14] A married couple can no longer think of themselves as pure individuals. The two are now, in a very real sense, one. Not mere partners, but existing mutually "one for the other."[15] In that oneness, they reflect Christ and the church—also a permanent bond. This metaphysical truth leads then to an ethical norm, that since the relationship mirrors the one between Christ and the church, they should then treat each other as Christ does the church, with self-sacrificial love. It is not an ephemeral fondness but a committed, lifelong love of giving oneself for the other.

---

13. Hays, *Moral Vision*, 351.

14. This is not to say that *sex* is the foundation of marriage but that the one flesh that is created through this relationship, with sex as an integral component, is the foundation.

15. Farley, *Just Love*, 133–34.

Is Consent Enough?

Consent is the word of our day. It is a good word, a necessary one, in a world rampant with cases of sexual assault; but it is not enough. In essence, the ethic of consent says that any sex between two consenting adults is ethical. How consent is defined has changed throughout the years as needs have become more apparent. The mantra "no means no" is ubiquitous, while "yes means yes" has more recently begun gaining steam. The latter gets at the need to not just avoid a no from a potential partner but that they should "enthusiastically consent" to the sexual encounter for it to be ethical.[16] While consent is certainly necessary in a good sexual ethic, it is not sufficient. These changing standards on what counts as consent reveal the murkiness of the situation. Consent depends on complex personal relations, with varying power dynamics and social expectations. "Sex is complex; consent treats it like a problem of arithmetic."[17] Arithmetic that is impossible to calculate. What comes from it is a world where many are left with sexual encounters that may have been consented to but fail to be good.

The journalist Christine Emba, after interviewing a number of sexually active young people on the subject, puts it like this: "Young Americans are engaging in sexual encounters they don't really want for reasons they don't fully agree with. . . . The outcome is a world in which young people are both liberated *and* miserable. While college scandals and the #MeToo moment may have cemented a baseline rule for how to get into bed with someone without crossing legal lines, that hasn't made the experience of dating and finding a partner simple or satisfying. Instead, the experience is often sad, unsettling, even traumatic."[18] She argues the problem is that consent is helpful as a legal requirement but not as an ethical standard. We need something more for sex to not only be legal but to be good. This is illustrated in several accounts from women she interviewed, who testify that they consented to a given sexual encounter, but by the end it felt off, maybe even wrong somehow.

In the end, Emba concludes that consent is an incredibly low bar:

> Even the newer, qualified versions of consent—the "affirmative," the "enthusiastic," still have that as their baseline question: "Did I

16. For an account of a college campus wrestling with how to teach (and regulate) consent to their students, see Grinberg, "Schools Preach 'Enthusiastic' Yes."

17. Emba, *Rethinking Sex*, 7.

18. Emba, "Consent Is Not Enough," lines 32–37.

get permission of the right kind, so that what I am going to do to this person is not statedly against their will?" The modifiers may try to complicate the question, but they're most often perceived as simply shifting the goalposts—rather than stopping when your partner says no, you now have to get them to say yes. But the end goal is still to Get the Sex from someone else without having committed an actual violation. If we invoke just getting consent as an ideal—the ideal, the highest ethical standard for any encounter—we're giving ourselves a pass on the hard but meaningful questions: whether that consent was fairly gotten, what our partners actually want, whether we even should be doing what we've gotten consent to do.[19]

This final question is anathema to our consumeristic culture, yet reveals an inherent problem with hookup sexuality. It sees the other person essentially as someone from whom I am trying to get something. In this context, sex is not a way to mutually and selflessly love one another but one where I use you to attain the end of my own pleasure. No wonder women feel "used" in these encounters, as that is exactly what is happening—turning sex into a consumeristic enterprise, where one literally shops for the next bit of pleasure. Margaret Farley points out that Kant argued for traditional sexual mores on precisely this basis. "In his *Lecture on Ethics* he introduced a justification for marriage not in terms of procreation but of altruistic love, arguing that only a mutual commitment in marriage can save sexual desire from making a sexual partner into a mere means to one's own pleasure."[20]

A Marriage Ethic?

Christians often stop there, saying simply that as long as one waits until marriage, sex is good. Yet this approach also fails to meet Christlike standards of goodness, for a couple reasons. First, it conceives marriage as just another way to get what you want: sex. While marriage is certainly the best context for sex, it should not be seen merely as a means to it. Marriage is a life of committed, self-giving love, not a method to secure our own desires. Second, just because a couple is married does not mean that every sexual encounter they have is morally good. One still must act in Christlike love

19. Emba, *Rethinking Sex*, 16–17.
20. Farley, *Just Love*, 52.

for it to be ethical. And finally, the emphasis on marriage also ignores the many ways we become mastered by sexual desire without actually engaging in sexual intercourse. Marriage itself, then, cannot be the Christian sexual ethic.

Interestingly, and surprising to some, the Bible never explicitly says one must wait to be married to have sex. Given its context, it wouldn't need to. People got married relatively young. Scripture just assumes that sex and marriage go together. This assumption, though, is rooted not only in cultural norms but also in the design of creation, where two are to become one flesh. What we ultimately glean from this "one flesh" teaching, and the surrounding teaching from Jesus, is that marriage is the ideal context for sex. It creates an environment where two people can engage in the eminently vulnerable act of sexual intercourse, giving themselves over for the sake of the other, in complete acceptance and affirmation. In an environment of lifelong commitment, it avoids the consumeristic nature of sex outside of marriage. One does not need to perform for the other to win them over, they have already been accepted and promised love. The sexual act also feeds into the marriage itself, fueling desire for one's spouse, and reaffirming one's love and acceptance of the other, encouraging that lifelong commitment.

Our ethic is not marriage but the cruciform Christ, who calls us, in our sexuality, to not be mastered by anything and to imitate his self-giving love. This path can then be beautifully and healthily worked out in a one-flesh union, where two become one in a marriage of mind, body, and spirit, for the duration of their lives. This union gives them the freedom to be vulnerable without fear, to love without restraint, and to be secure in their belovedness.

Christocentric Ethic of Love

What, then, do we say to our young people, asking whether they have to wait until marriage to have sex? The answer, it seems, is fourfold: (1) our ethic, even our sexual ethic, is founded on the crucified Christ, who models a self-giving love that refuses to objectify others but rather respects, even invigorates, their full humanity; (2) sex is life giving, beautiful, and powerful—and, in that power, can be dangerous; (3) sex is an act that creates an indissoluble bond with another in mind, body, and spirit; and (4) marriage is the best context to channel this powerful desire in a self-giving way, one that respects, and feeds into, the union created.

What, then, do we say to those same young people who have already had sex? Given our modern context, where people wait until their late twenties or thirties before getting married, the standard of "waiting until marriage" is increasingly difficult. Christians need to be honest about this reality and recognize that in this issue more often than others we must engage in ethics "in the middle," where boundaries are unclear, principles fail, and wisdom must be hard earned.

Fortunately, we have an example from Jesus to reenact in our own lives. In John we are told that some scribes and Pharisees bring a woman before Jesus and question him, "Teacher, this woman was caught in the very act of committing adultery. Now in the law Moses commanded us to stone such women. Now what do you say?"

He responds by writing some unknown words on the ground, then saying, "Let anyone among you who is without sin be the first to throw a stone at her." They walk away, one by one. He then turns to the woman and says, "Woman, where are they? Has no one condemned you?"

"No one, sir," she responds.

"Neither do I condemn you. Go your way, and from now on do not sin again" (John 8:4–11).

Jesus walks a delicate and life-giving balance in this exchange, one we would do well to emulate. He both recognizes sin as sin and refuses to condemn the sinner. He is not so much concerned with purity as with wholeness, and with a trajectory toward oneness with God. We are all fallen and in need of a savior—and that Savior has come. No matter what you have done, or what has been done to you, you are not irreversibly spoiled. No matter what you have done, or what has been done to you, you are infinitely and eternally loved by your Creator. No sin is greater than the grace of our Savior. Therefore, a sexual ethic with Christ at the center should not induce shame but hope. Through Christ, we have hope that we can be made whole. Through Christ, our sexuality can be the beautiful, life-giving reality it was always meant to be.

12

A Christocentric Political Ethic

THE GOSPEL IS INHERENTLY POLITICAL. We serve a King. As we have seen throughout this book, this King has a lot to say about our world and how we live in it. Our duty is to participate in the work of bringing his kingdom to earth. In order to do that, we must engage in politics, a sphere that affects nearly every aspect of our lives. This sphere, though, is one fraught with controversy, with strong opinions, and, unfortunately, a lot of poor theology dearly held. In this chapter we lay the groundwork for a political ethic with Jesus as its Thesis. You will notice that specific issues are not discussed. This is because we believe that Christians can hold many varying political opinions and that, at times, it may not be clear what a Jesus-lensed political ethic should produce—he did not have much to say about economic regulation, after all. Disagreement, then, is inevitable—the result of kindhearted Christians of all types pursuing the good of their neighbor. What we cannot disagree on, though, is that Jesus is our King, and our allegiance is to him and to him alone. This fact will produce a few general themes we believe are essential to any Christ-centered politic ethic—that our primary citizenship is in heaven, our primary identity is in Christ, our primary task is taking care of our neighbor, and our primary end is justice.

Our Primary Citizenship Is in Heaven

In Philippians, shortly after the *kenosis* passage, Paul challenges his readers to join him in following Christ. He tells them, "For, as I have often told you before and now tell you again even with tears, many live as enemies of the cross of Christ. Their destiny is destruction, their god is their stomach, and their glory is in their shame. Their mind is set on earthly things. But our citizenship is in heaven. And we eagerly await a savior from there, the Lord Jesus Christ, who, by the power that enables him to bring everything under his control, will transform our lowly bodies so that they will be like his glorious body" (Phil 3:18–21a). Our citizenship is in heaven, and our King is Jesus. Our allegiance is not to our country but to Christ. Recognizing this is the first step in a political ethic with Jesus as its Thesis.

As citizens of heaven our duty is first and foremost to our heavenly endeavors. Yet given God's incarnational nature, these heavenly endeavors have significant earthly import. Being a citizen of heaven does not mean we avoid earthly tasks, or ignore earthly problems; it means our earthly problems get solved in a heavenly way—a way that reflects the resurrection we see in Christ and look forward to in the eschaton. As we discussed in chapter 9, the resurrection of Jesus affirms physical reality and urges us to participate in resurrecting everything around us, something Christ will complete in the end. The hope of a seamless integration of heaven and earth is our guide. In other words, this future hope fuels our political action today.

This future hope, as noted in Revelation, is for "all tribes and peoples and languages." All will stand "before the throne and before the Lamb" (Rev 7:9). This heavenly kingdom has no borders. It is a global kingdom. When our politics become about us and our country to the detriment of others, we fail to live as true members of the kingdom of heaven. This may put us out of step with others in our country; it may leave us feeling somewhat alien; because, in the end, that is exactly what we are.

Our Primary Identity Is in Christ

In the last chapter we looked at a passage from 1 Corinthians where Paul corrects the Corinthians' misconception about their saved state. They believed that what they did with their bodies did not matter because their bodies would be destroyed in the end. Paul corrects them, writing that their bodies are "not meant for fornication but for the Lord, and the Lord for the body" (1 Cor 6:13b). He ends this passage telling them, "Or do you not know that your body is a temple of the Holy Spirit within you, which you have from God, and that you are not your own? For you were bought with a price; therefore glorify God in your body" (1 Cor 6:19–20). In the beginning, God dwelled with humanity in the garden. Then he dwelled with them in the tabernacle and the temple, then in the person of Jesus Christ.

Now, he dwells with us in our person. Our bodies are temples of the Holy Spirit. Therefore, we are not our own.[1]

In joining with Christ in death and life, we give ourselves completely over to him. The good news is that this relieves us of modern anxiety of identity formation—a process we engage in without end. As Alan Noble writes, this "is not a definitive action, it is an ongoing process. You're always journeying and never arriving. If you're responsible for meaning in your life, you can never cease the labor of creating and sustaining moments of significance. If you're responsible for defining and expressing your identity, you can never cease expressing, never cease discovering and fine-tuning your identity."[2] This never-ending search for the real you is an anxiety-inducing nightmare. Fortunately, in finding our identity in Christ, we are released from this labyrinth. It is not our responsibility to discover who we are on our own. We are formed into who we are in relationship with Christ. We become more truly ourselves only when we find ourselves in step with the one who created us, and in so doing, we find a life of peace. As Noble puts it, "to belong to Christ is to find existence in His grace."[3]

An identity in Christ includes recognizing him as our highest obligation, our sole allegiance, which means all other affiliations should be secondary.[4] Unfortunately, that is not what we find in most politics. A study by Stanford scholar Shanto Iyengar has shown that the strongest identity Americans hold is not race, ethnicity, or religion but their party, and that the strength of that partisan bond "has amplified the level of political polarization in the U.S."[5]—polarization affecting not only our political climate but our church pews. In the words of Daniel Silliman, in an article from *Christianity Today*, "the problem of polarization, according to pastors of purple churches struggling to minister to red Republicans and blue Democrats during another divisive election, is that people stop fighting. They part ways. And they sort themselves by political preference. Polarization makes

1. For an excellent book-length reflection on this concept, see Noble, *You Are Not Your Own*

2. Noble, *You Are Not Your Own*, 83.

3. Noble, *You Are Not Your Own*, 5.

4. Matthew W. Bates makes a persuasive argument in *Salvation by Allegiance Alone*, that "'faith' and 'belief,' insofar as they serve as overarching terms to describe what brings about eternal salvation, should be excised from Christian discourse." He argues that *allegiance* is a much more fitting term for what the New Testament teaches brings about salvation in Christ (Bates, *Salvation by Allegiance Alone*, 3).

5. Martinovich, "Americans' Partisan Identities," lines 9–10.

it seem like unity in Christ can only come after political unity. Polarization makes it seem like partisanship is stronger than the gospel."[6] The troubling truth is, in the hearts of most American Christians, it is.

Iyengar found that one reason for the strong ties to partisan identity "is that—unlike race, religion and gender, where social norms dictate behavior—there are few, if any, constraints on the expression of hostility toward people who adhere to opposing political ideologies."[7] While there are words and attitudes considered inappropriate when directed toward someone of the opposite race or gender, there are no boundaries regarding those with opposing political ideologies. Our political leaders encourage that kind of behavior, often exhibiting it themselves. So not only does polarization increase the hostility we feel toward our neighbor, but we cling to party affiliation in part as an outlet for our hatred.

Finding our identity in Christ means rejecting every aspect of this horrid paradigm. It means refusing to see our neighbor as our enemy, no matter how much they disagree. It means disavowing fear and hate, even when we see things are not going our way. It means finding hope not in political power but in the eschatological promise of Christ. This will require a total reorientation for many of us, engaging in the process of reforming our theological foundations outside of the political sphere, so we can then reenter it with fresh perspective, recognizing that if we always agree with one side, we probably haven't done the work.

Brian Brock writes, "Christian ethics must continually combat its tendency to collapse into either a simplistic validation of cultural presuppositions or a blanket reaction against them." To avoid this, Brock argues that "Christian theology must constantly seek to clarify how God generates a community that has its own ethos, distinct and distinctly Christian. How does the church begin to see itself as 'other' than the world?"[8] We are not of this world; our identity in Christ will often leave us on the outside looking in. Yet this distinctiveness is what makes us a corrective to our culture. We are not meant to be kings but prophets, urging those around us to follow the way of the one true King. No matter our political persuasion, there will be times our preferred party goes against the way of Christ. In those moments, it is our duty to call them out. There will also be times when our ill-favored party is in line with the way of Christ. In those moments, it is

6. Silliman, "At Purple Churches," lines 10–16.

7. Martinovich, "Americans' Partisan Identities," lines 30–35.

8. Brock, *Singing Ethos of God*, 281.

our duty to cheer them on. All of this requires wisdom, doing our best to navigate our modern world with the mind of Christ; and it requires humility, recognizing the difficulty of that task.

In choosing to follow Christ, we are admitting we are wrong on a fundamental level—wrong and in need of a savior. Repentance is a way of life, readily accepting the ways we are erred, constantly seeking truth and forgiveness. Intellectual humility should naturally flow from this foundation. There is nothing wrong with being confident in what we believe. Where we go wrong is when we assume others are stupid or immoral for disagreeing, when we demonize or ostracize them, or when we refuse to entertain new and different ideas. Intellectual humility is a form of wisdom. The goal is to find the right place between close-minded stubbornness and gullibility. It is also a form of virtue, not necessarily about how often one changes their mind but how graciously they welcome new ideas and new people. Another way to look at intellectual humility is to imagine its opposite, in the form of intellectual pride. We go wrong when we desire being "in the know" above an honest search for truth. The conspiratorial thinking that emerges from this lacks the virtue necessary in Christlike reasoning. Finding our identity in Christ should motivate us to love even when we disagree and to be ready to admit when we're wrong. He is our King, the only one who knows all things and purely desires our good.

Our Primary Task Is Taking Care of Our Neighbor

In chapter 9 we referenced Martin Luther King Jr., and it is worth revisiting that quotation: "Any religion that professes to be concerned about the souls of men and is not concerned about the slums that damn them, the economic conditions that strangle them and the social conditions that cripple them is a spiritually moribund religion awaiting burial."[9] In that chapter we discussed the temptation many Christians have to disembody the faith, to make it about a heaven that happens to us, sometime in the future, rather than a heaven we participate in bringing to earth right now. King reminds us that we must care about the conditions of life today, because that is what it means to love our neighbor. Given the nature of our government and its effects on the economic and social conditions of our neighbors, we must then care about politics.

9. King, *Strength to Love*, 160–61.

This motivation, of care for neighbor, puts politics in its proper place. It is not about gaining power or looking out for our own self-interest. When politics becomes for us the game it so often is, it ceases to be Christian. As those who find our identity in Christ, politics can never become about us and our power. This identity goes against so much of what politics often becomes, because rather than acquiring power, we are called to give it up. Our task is always the one Christ embodied, self-sacrifice for the other. When entering the voting booth, the question is never "What will be best for me?" but "What will be best for my neighbor?" In the short term, this may mean "our" issues do not win the day. But in the long term, it will mean we were faithful to Christ, and he will be faithful to us in bringing about a more just world. After all, we could never ensure a just world on our own; that was never our job. Our task is to participate in our King's process of re-creation. It is something he ensures, not us. We need not fear.

Our Primary End Is Justice

Participating in the story of Christ means working toward the eventual end where all is set right. Christ has stretched that eventual era backward, overlapping it with the era of death, and we work to do the same, bringing light to the dark world around us. The prevailing theme of that eventual era is justice, what it looks like when things are set right—between God, humanity, and the rest of creation—and it is tied together closely with the idea of righteousness. Justice and righteousness appear together frequently in the Old Testament. In Jer 22:3, for example, the author writes, "Thus says the LORD: Act with justice and righteousness, and deliver from the hand of the oppressor anyone who has been robbed. And do no wrong or violence to the alien, the orphan, and the widow, or shed innocent blood in this place." And Ps 146:7–9 describes the Lord God who "executes justice for the oppressed; who gives food to the hungry. The LORD sets the prisoners free; the LORD opens the eyes of the blind. The LORD lifts up those who are bowed down; the Lord loves the righteous . . . but the way of the wicked he brings to ruin." To live righteously in society entails the pursuit of justice, and justice looks like working for the good of the oppressed.

As we saw in chapter 7, this is also how Jesus saw his own mission in life. In Luke, when announcing his ministry, he quoted from Isaiah saying, "The Spirit of the Lord is on me, because he has anointed me to proclaim good news to the poor. He has sent me to proclaim freedom for the prisoners and recovery of sight for the blind, to set the oppressed free, to proclaim the year of the Lord's favor" (Luke 4:18). Elsewhere in Isaiah, God speaks to his people, reprimanding them for ignoring justice in pursuit of false piety. Chapter 58 includes a powerful and scathing rebuke. God tells his prophet to "announce to my people their rebellion." "Day after day they seek me and delight to know my ways, as if they were a nation that practiced righteousness and did not forsake the ordinance of their God." They want to know why God appears to not be listening, why their nation is in strife. God responds, "Look, you serve your own interest on your fast day, and oppress all your workers. Look, you fast only to quarrel and to fight and to strike with a wicked fist." They fast while the needy go unheard. They fast and continue in violence. Mere worship of God does not matter if the work of God is not completed. God tells them, "Is not this the fast I choose: to loose the bonds of injustice, to undo the thongs of the yoke, to let the oppressed go free, and to break every yoke? Is it not to share your bread with the hungry, and bring the homeless poor into your house; when you see the naked, to cover them, and not to hide yourself from your own kin?" When this happens, he tells them, "Then your light shall break forth like the dawn, and your healing shall spring up quickly" (Isa 58:1–12).

This is the work of the church in politics, and beyond. It is to care for the poor, the oppressed, the unheard—to speak on their behalf and work toward lifting them up. Using whatever resources we have, whether inside the political sphere or out, God commands us to pursue justice.

The prophets, Isaiah being one, are a great resource for thinking about the church's role in society. They were God's voice to the nation, so it makes sense to look to them for how he thinks a nation should function. In his study of the biblical prophets, Abraham Joshua Heschel, a Jewish philosopher and rabbi who walked alongside Martin Luther King Jr. at Selma, wrote:

> The prophet is a man who feels fiercely. God has thrust a burden upon his shoulder, and he is bowed and stunned at man's fierce greed. Frightful is the agony of man; no human voice can convey its full terror. Prophecy is the voice that God has lent to the silent agony, a voice to the plundered poor, to the profaned riches of the world. It is a form of living, a crossing point of God and man. God is raging in the prophet's words.[10]

10. Heschel, *Prophets*, 5–6.

According to Jewish tradition, the prophets speak on behalf of God. They feel deeply the needs of the people. They see the greed, the oppression, the agony, and are compelled to raise their voices against it. They are not concerned about appearances and are often mocked because of it. The weight of the oppressed is on them, and they can do nothing but speak. They comfort in crisis, assuring that God's will will be done. Yet in that assurance there is a warning to the oppressor, because in setting things right, they will be brought low.[11] Heschel writes, "In a sense, the calling of the prophet may be described as that of an advocate or champion, speaking for those who are too weak to plead their own cause."[12]

The prophets are so committed to the care of the oppressed because they have an altered view of justice. Americans often think of justice as each person getting what they deserve. A criminal commits a crime, justice means he is punished. A person works hard, they get what they earned. The iconic image of our legal system is Lady Justice, holding a scale (perfectly balanced) in one hand and a sword in the other. Heschel argues that, in a Jewish image, the sword would disappear, and the scales would be uneven—tipped in favor of the oppressed. As Heschel writes, "There is a point at which strict justice is unjust."[13] That is because the point of biblical justice is not to give to each what they deserve but to make all things right. Sometimes, giving someone what they do not deserve will bring about a better world. In fact, that is exactly what the story of Jesus reveals. In giving grace, Jesus fails to render us what we are due but, in so doing, brings about a new and better creation. A Christocentric political ethic demands that we do the same for the world around us.

Political ethics, like all ethics, requires wisdom. We have an end to which we are striving (justice) and a model for how to get there (the person of Jesus, our King), but it is our duty to work out the details—navigating, in grace, our increasingly complex world with the help of the Holy Spirit, in fellowship with the body of Christ.

The Cross

In Phil 3, Paul presents a fascinating argument. The end of verse 18 and beginning of 19 are a surprising set of statements—"many live as enemies

11. Gorman, *Reading Revelation Responsibly*, 35.

12. Heschel, *Prophets*, 261.

13. Heschel, *Prophets*, 275.

of the cross of Christ. Their destiny is destruction" (NIV). The cross was a device of death, a tool of execution. Yet those living as enemies of the cross are the ones destined for destruction. The cross Paul speaks of, though, is the cross of Christ, the one used to bring a defeat to death through self-giving love, giving hope to all those who live in step with his way. It is a way that challenges us to love our neighbor (near and far) through the establishment of justice and to live in hope rather than fear. Living as an enemy of that cross, in pursuit of our own gain, fearing our loss of power, *will* end in destruction. This pursuit of power, with fear as tool and guide, is a political ethic too often employed. As followers of Christ, we can choose not to engage in that death-dealing endeavor and commit to let the cross be our guide. In the end, our country, and our world, will be better for it.

Conclusion

Who do you say I am?

—JESUS CHRIST

FROM THE INTRODUCTION OF our book, throughout each section, each chapter and each thought, we have held to one Thesis, Jesus. This is not a flippant religious statement to us either. We have wholeheartedly and honestly endeavored to present a lucid, rational, pragmatic, thoughtful, Christocentric faith—a faith that is tethered to and inextricably linked with the person of Jesus. He is the incomparable person who has had an indelible impact upon every aspect of history and the entirety of humanity. At least, we think so. We have also asserted that he is undoubtedly and undeniably the focal point of the Christian faith. We think that he is the glue. Yes, a vortex he is, in and of himself. We have asserted that he is the centrifugal force that ultimately draws all things together. However, we didn't write this book for ourselves. We wrote it for Jesus, because we are so very convinced that he is the Thesis. We are also convinced that he wanted for us to write it for you, our reader, in an effort to prod, poke, and provoke you to consider and respond to his timeless and reverberating question:

"Who do you say that I am?"

And then, once you have answered, hopefully, once you have submitted to Jesus, the One who is the Thesis, you will live a life of faith, built upon him, tethered to him, empowered by his Spirit to live a life where he actually lives as the Thesis, through you.

In part 1, we asserted that he is the Thesis by being the actual fulfillment of the true myth. He is the One who helps all the partially true cosmologies and stories make some sense. They were partial truths wrapped up in fictional myths. Jesus, on the other hand, was the One who came in

131

real space and time, according to the truth of Scripture and launched the story of God into reality. At least, we believe that he did. But who do you say that he is?

In part 2, we asserted that Jesus is in fact presented in every book of the Bible and is undeniably the Thesis to which they all ultimately point. A Thesis that would become a miraculous Seed of faith, prophesied by the mouth of God himself in Gen 3:14–15. Then, at the perfect time, that prophesied Seed, the Seed of the Woman, would engage in a deadly battle with the seed of the serpent—a battle that would ensue throughout the millennia. However, by living a perfect life and fulfilling all that had to be done on man's behalf, the Seed of the woman would finally crush the head of the serpent at the place of the skull, Golgotha. Then, after delivering that crushing blow, he would resurrect on the third day, sending his Spirit to empower his subjects to proclaim his victory. The serpent was crushed. Long live the King. At least, that's what we believe about him. But who do you say that he is?

In part 3, we examined in depth, the multifaceted nature of the Thesis himself. How he was and is the Thesis, because he was and is fully God and fully man. We considered how he was and is the One who announced the initiation of a new Kingdom and how we might act as his subjects. We considered that he was and is the Healer—the One whose very name possesses healing ramifications and powers. Powers that heal both body and soul, temporally and eternally. His is a name that propels his followers to imitate him and bring his healing to others as well. We considered his nature as a deity who welcomed the outcast. Never before has there been a deity like him. One who incessantly bids his followers to emulate him and reach for the lost, the broken, and the disenfranchised on his behalf. We considered the anxiety that he faced as a result of all these things. The fact that in his humanity, he would be encumbered with every emotion, temptation, and trial that would haunt humankind yet face them victoriously, not being mastered by them. He would in fact master them by submitting to a brutal death, then resurrecting from the dead on the third day. Although there have been stories of fictitious gods who did some of these things, Jesus did them actually and factually. His nature is unique, perfect and untarnished; and he offers that nature to any who would submit to him as Thesis and Lord of their lives. At least, that's what we believe. But who do you say that he is?

In part 4, we examined ways to practically apply Jesus as Thesis into the warp and woof of our personal human existence. What does a Christocentric ethic actually look like in one's day-to-day life? How might it affect our actions and our thoughts? Two primary areas were examined. First, especially in the hypersexualized culture in which we exist today, was the area of sexuality. How might Jesus be Lord of our sexuality? The fourfold ethic of love that we established, should not be forgotten: (1) our ethic, even our sexual ethic, is founded on the crucified Christ, who models a self-giving love that refuses to objectify others but rather respects, even invigorates, their full humanity; (2) sex is life giving, beautiful, and powerful—and in that power, can be dangerous; (3) sex is an act that creates an indissoluble bond with another, in mind, body, and spirit; and (4) marriage is the best context to channel this powerful desire in a self-giving way, one that respects, and feeds into, the union created. A sexual ethic empowered by the Spirit and based upon these understandings is regenerative to individuals and cultures alike. We proposed that Jesus, being the resurrected Lord, has garnered the right to speak into and direct us in every aspect of our bodies, especially in regard to sex. At least, we believe that he is Lord of our sexuality. But who do you say that he is?

The second area of application to life and human existence was the area of politics. Politically, Jesus was and never will be a member of a political party. He was, is, and forever will be a King. There are no votes regarding this. The members of the Holy Trinity voted long ago, and Jesus is King. Therefore, the political positions of his subjects should be the ones that he espouses. However, as we noted, politics in relation to his subjects can be a challenging issue. It has been so for thousands of years and will most probably remain the same. His subjects have been known to differ in their opinions on various issues, both inside and outside of the political spectrum. We believe that our primary identity is in Christ, with our citizenship residing in heaven. Within that context, we believe, according to the teachings of our King, that our primary task is taking care of our neighbor and our primary end is justice. We must especially be unified in these things, always understanding that there is one Lord, one faith, one God and Father of all and that he has expressed himself most fully in the person of King Jesus. At least, these are the things that we believe. But what do you believe? Who do you say that he is? While there are a myriad of other areas that might be considered, we felt that considering these would empower you to begin to follow the King and grow in your knowledge of how to do so more fully. Regardless of the issue, we believe that as Thesis, resurrected Lord, and King, he has the sole right to speak into all areas of human existence. Consider yourself challenged to submit to him, follow him, talk about him, study his words, and ask for his help to do the same.

While the following quote from C. S. Lewis has been oft misquoted, we're going to do so deliberately, adding our changes in emboldened italics. We do so because we believe that the changes stay within the spirit of what Lewis was saying and especially align with the Thesis of this work.

"I believe in Christianity [*Christ*] as I believe that the Sun has risen, not only because I see it [*him*] but because by it [*him*], I see everything else."[1]

---

1. "Is Theology Poetry?," in Lewis, *Weight of Glory*, 140.

Bibliography

119 Ministries. "The Hebrew Root of Amen." YouTube, May 22, 2017. https://www. youtube.com/watch?reload =9&v=3fko7gir6Hw.

Athanasius. *On the Incarnation: The Treatise "De Incarnatione Verbi Dei."* Crestwood, NY: St. Vladimir's Seminary Press, 1998.

Bates, Matthew W. *Salvation by Allegiance Alone: Rethinking Faith, Works, and the Gospel of Jesus the King.* Grand Rapids: Baker Academic, 2017.

Bonhoeffer, Dietrich. *Christ the Center.* Translated by Edwin Robertson. New York: Harper & Row, 1978.

———. *Ethics.* Edited by Clifford J. Green. Dietrich Bonhoeffer Works—Reader's Edition. Minneapolis: Fortress, 2015.

———. *Meditating on the Word.* Edited and translated by David McI. Gracie. 2nd ed. Cambridge, MA: Cowley, 2000.

Bourne, Ella. "The Messianic Prophecy in Vergil's Fourth Eclogue." *Classical Journal* 11 (Apr. 1916) 390–400. https://www.jstor.org/stable/pdf/3287925.pdf.

Brawley, Robert L. "Luke." In *The New Testament*, edited by Margaret P. Aymer et al., 217–64. Fortress Commentary on the Bible. Minneapolis: Fortress, 2014.

Bray, Olive, ed. and trans. *The Elder or Poetic Edda, Commonly Known as Saemund's Edda: Part 1. The Mythological Poems.* London: Kings Weighhouse Club, 1908.

Britannica, T. Editors of Encylopedia. "Nicene Creed." Revised and updated by Melissa Petruzzello. *Encylopedia Britannica*, May 15, 2020. https://www.britannica.com/ topic/Nicene-Creed.

Brock, Brian. *Singing the Ethos of God: On the Place of Christian Ethics in Scripture.* Grand Rapids: Eerdmans, 2007.

Carpenter, Humphrey. *The Inklings: C. S. Lewis, J. R. R. Tolkien, Charles Williams and Their Friends.* Hammersmith, UK: HarperCollins, 2006.

Carter, Warren. *Seven Events That Shaped the New Testament World.* Grand Rapids: Baker Academic, 2013.

Chesterton, G. K. *The Everlasting Man.* San Francisco, CA: Ignatius, 1993.

Cicero. *Ethical Writings of Cicero.* Translated by Andrew P. Peabody. Boston: Little, Brown, 1887.

Clements, Ronald E. "Proverbs." In *Eerdmans Commentary on the Bible*, edited by James D. G. Dunn et al., 438. Grand Rapids: Eerdmans, 2003.

Confucius. *The Analects of Confucius.* Translated by Arthur Waley. London: Allen & Unwin, 1956.

CT Editors. "The 50 Countries Where It's Most Dangerous to Follow Jesus in 2021." *Christianity Today*, Jan. 13, 2021. https://www.christianitytoday.com/news/2021/january/christian-persecution-2021-countries-open-doors-watch-list.html.

Currid, John. "Introduction to Biblical Theology." Lecture notes, Reformed Theological Seminary, Charlotte, NC, 2003.

Douglas, Kelly Brown. *What's Faith Got to Do with It? Black Bodies/Christian Souls.* Maryknoll, NY: Orbis, 2005.

Dunn, James D. G., and J. W. Rogerson, eds. *Eerdmans Commentary on the Bible.* Grand Rapids: Eerdmans, 2003.

Duriez, Colin. *Tolkein and C. S. Lewis: The Gift of Friendship.* Mahwah, NJ: Hidden Spring, 2003.

Eldredge, John. *Epic: The Story God Is Telling.* Nashville: Thomas Nelson, 2004.

Emba, Christine. "Consent Is Not Enough." *Washington Post*, Mar. 17, 2022. https://www.washingtonpost.com/opinions/2022/03/17/sex-ethics-rethinking-consent-culture/.

———. *Rethinking Sex: A Provocation.* New York: Sentinel, 2022.

Epictetus. *Epictetus: The Discourses as Reported by Arrian, the Manual, and Fragments.* Translated by W. A. Oldfather. 2 vols. Loeb Classical Library. Cambridge, MA: Harvard University Press, 1961.

Farley, Margaret A. *Just Love: A Framework for Christian Sexual Ethics.* New York: Continuum International, 2006.

Fee, Gordon D. *The First Epistle to the Corinthians.* Rev. ed. New International Commentary on the New Testament. Grand Rapids: Eerdmans, 2014.

Fiddes, Paul S. *Past Event and Present Salvation: The Christian Idea of Atonement.* Louisville: Westminster/John Knox, 1989.

———. "Salvation." In *The Oxford Handbook of Systematic Theology*, edited by John B. Webster et al., 176–96. Oxford Handbooks. Oxford, UK: Oxford University Press, 2009.

French, Nancy. "Survivors, Ex-employees Say Unreported Abuse at Kanakuk Camps in Branson Spans Decades." *Springfield News-Leader*, May 26, 2022; updated May 28, 2022. https://www.news-leader.com/story/news/local/ozarks/2022/05/26/kanakuk-kamps-abuse-unreported-decades-victims-say-missouri-pete-newman/9803409002/.

Glynn, Patrick. *God: The Evidence: The Reconciliation of Faith and Reason in a Postsecular World.* Rocklin, CA: Prima, 1997.

Gonzalez, Justo L. *The Early Church to the Reformation.* Vol. 1 of *The Story of Christianity.* New York: HarperCollins, 2010.

Gorman, Michael J. *Inhabiting the Cruciform God: Kenosis, Justification, and Theosis in Paul's Narrative Soteriology.* Grand Rapids: Eerdmans, 2009.

———. *Reading Revelation Responsibly: Uncivil Worship and Witness; Following the Lamb into the New Creation.* Eugene, OR: Cascade, 2011.

Green, Chris E. W. *All Things Beautiful: An Aesthetic Christology.* Waco, TX: Baylor University Press, 2021.

———. *Sanctifying Interpretation: Vocation, Holiness, and Scripture.* Cleveland, TN: CPT, 2015.

Grinberg, Emanuella. "Schools Preach 'Enthusiastic' Yes in Sex Consent Education." *CNN*, Sept. 3, 2014. https://www.cnn.com/2014/09/03/living/affirmative-consent-school-policy/.

Hall, H. R. *The Ancient History of the Near East from the Earliest Times to the Battle of Salamis.* New York: MacMillan, 1913.

Hamilton, James. "The Skull Crushing Seed of the Woman: Inner-Biblical Interpretation of Genesis 3:15." *Southern Baptist Journal of Theology* 10 (2006) 30–54. https://jimhamilton.info/wp-content/uploads/2008/04/hamilton_sbjt_10-2.pdf.

Hastings, James, et al., eds. *Encyclopaedia of Religion and Ethics.* 10 vols. New York: Scribner's, 1961.

Hauerwas, Stanley. *Matthew.* Brazos Theological Commentary on the Bible. Grand Rapids: Brazos, 2013.

Hays, Richard B. *First Corinthians.* Interpretation, a Bible Commentary for Teaching and Preaching. Louisville: Westminister John Knox Press, 2011.

———. *The Moral Vision of the New Testament: Community, Cross, New Creation: A Contemporary Introduction to New Testament Ethics.* San Francisco: HarperSanFrancisco, 1996.

Heaney, Seamus. *Beowulf: A Verse Translation.* Edited by Daniel Donoghue. Norton Critical Edition. New York: Norton, 2002.

Heschel, Abraham Joshua. *The Prophets.* Perennial Classics. New York: Perennial, 2001.

Homer. "The *Iliad* of Homer." In *Greek Literature,* edited by Paul MacKendrick and Herbert Howe, translated by Alston H. Chase and William G. Perry Jr., vol. 1 of *Classics in Translation,* 13–48. Madison: University of Wisconsin Press, 1952.

Janet, Paul. *Histoire de la Science Politique dans ses Rapports avec la Morale.* Vol. 1. Paris: Alcan, 1887.

Juvenal. *Juvenal: For Schools.* Edited and translated by John E. B. Mayor. London: MacMillan, 1879.

Keller, Timothy. *King's Cross: The Story of the World in the Life of Jesus.* London: Hodder & Stoughton, 2013.

———. *The Reason for God: Belief in an Age of Skepticism.* New York: Penguin Group, 2008.

King, Martin Luther, Jr. *Strength to Love.* King Legacy Series. Boston: Beacon, 2019.

Lewis, C. S. *The Abolition of Man.* New York: HarperCollins, 1974.

———. *Books, Broadcasts, and the War 1931–1949.* Vol. 2 of *The Collected Letters of C. S. Lewis.* Edited by Walter Hooper. San Francisco: HarperCollins, 2004.

———. *The Grand Miracle: And Other Selected Essays on Theology and Ethics from God in the Dock.* Edited by Walter Hooper. New York: Ballantine, 1988.

———. *Mere Christianity.* San Francisco: HarperCollins, 2001.

———. *Miracles.* New York: Macmillan, 1960.

———. "Myth Became Fact." In *God in the Dock: Essays on Theology and Ethics,* edited by Walter Hooper, 63–67. Grand Rapids: Eerdmans, 1970.

———. *Of Other Worlds: Essays and Stories.* Edited by Walter Hooper. London: Bles, 1966.

———. *The Problem of Pain.* New York,: HarperOne, 2009.

———. *They Stand Together: The Letters of C. S. Lewis to Arthur Greeves (1914–1963).* Edited by Walter Hooper. New York: Collier/Macmillan, 1986.

———. *The Voyage of the Dawn Treader.* New York: HarperTrophy, 2005.

———. *The Weight of Glory: And Other Addresses.* New York: HarperCollins, 2001.

Loader, William R. G. *Sexuality in the New Testament: Understanding the Key Texts.* Louisville: Westminster John Knox Press, 2010.

Lockridge, S. M. "That's My King." YouTube, posted Jan. 12, 2012. https://youtu.be/4BhI4JKACUs.

MacDonald, George. *Phantastes: A Faerie Romance*. Grand Rapids: Eerdmans, 2021.

Marshall, Taylor. "Golgotha: The Word Symbolizes a Beautiful Reality!" *Taylor Marshall*, Mar. 28, 2013. https://taylormarshall.com/2013/03/golgotha-word-symbolizes-beautiful.html.

Martinez-Olivieri, Jules. "Jules Martinez-Olivieri—Christology, Liberation, Participation." OnScript, Feb., 2021. Podcast, 01:04:28. https://onscript.study/podcast/jules-martinez-olivieri-christology-liberation-participation/.

Martinovich, Milenko. "Americans' Partisan Identities Are Stronger Than Race and Ethnicity, Stanford Scholar Finds." Stanford News Service, Aug. 31, 2017. https://news.stanford.edu/press-releases/2017/08/31/political-party-er-race-religion/.

McCabe, Herbert. *Law, Love and Language*. London: Continuum, 2009.

McGrath, Allister. *C. S. Lewis: A Life; Eccentric Genius, Reluctant Prophet*. Colorado Springs, CO: Tyndale, 2013.

Menzies, James W. *True Myth: C. S. Lewis and Joseph Campbell on the Veracity of Christianity*. Eugene, OR: Pickwick, 2014.

Mercier, Hugo, and Dan Sperber. *The Enigma of Reason*. Cambridge, MA: Harvard University Press, 2017.

Moltmann, Jürgen. *Jesus Christ for Today's World*. Minneapolis: Fortress, 1994.

Noble, Alan. *You Are Not Your Own: Belonging to God in an Inhuman World*. Downers Grove, IL: InterVarsity, 2021.

Otto, Rudolf. *The Idea of the Holy*. London: Oxford University Press, 1958.

Plantinga, Alvin. *Warranted Christain Belief*. New York: Oxford University Press, 2000.

Polanyi, Michael. *Science, Faith, and Society: A Searching Examination of Meaning and Nature of Scientific Inquiry*. Chicago: University of Chicago Press, 1946.

Richardson, Don. *Eternity in Their Hearts: Startling Evidence of Belief in the One True God in Hundreds of Cultures throughout the World*. Bloomington, MN: Baker, 1981.

Roberts, Alexander, et al., eds. "The Encyclical Epistle of the Church at Smyrna: Concerning the Martyrdom of the Holy Polycarp." In vol. 1 of *The Anti-Nicene Fathers*, 39–44. New York: Cosimo Classics, 2007.

Roberts, Oral. *The Fourth Man*. Tulsa, OK: Oral Roberts, 1960.

Robinson, Laura. "There's a live possibility that Christ might function more as 'crown prince' (going to be king but not yet). But I think the question is less. . . ." Twitter post. Nov. 15, 2021. https://twitter.com/laurarbnsn/status/1460348733401575427?s=21.

Schaeffer, Francis A. *He Is There and He Is Not Silent*. Huemoz, CH: Schaeffer, 1972.

Shellnut, Kate. "Southern Baptists Refused to Act on Abuse, Despite Secret List of Pastors." *Christianity Today*, May 22, 2022. "Souther https://www.christianitytoday.com/news/2022/may/southern-baptist-abuse-investigation-sbc-ec-legal-survivors.html.

Shenk, Rick. "David and Goliath—Think Again!" Bethlehem College and Seminary, Nov. 9, 2018. https://bcsmn.edu/david-and-goliath/.

Silliman, Daniel. "At Purple Churches, Pastors Struggle with Polarized Congregations." *Christianity Today*, Oct. 20, 2020. https://www.christianitytoday.com/ct/2020/november/purple-church-political-polarization-unity-identity-christ.html.

———, and Kate Shellnut. "Ravi Zacharias Hid Hundreds of Pictures of Women, Abuse during Massages, and a Rape Allegation." *Christianity Today*, Feb. 11, 2021. https://

www.christianitytoday.com/news/2021/february/ravi-zacharias-rzim-investigation-sexual-abuse-sexting-rape.html.

Simeon, Charles. "Discourse 7: The Seed of the Woman." Biblia Plus, n.d. https://www.bibliaplus.org/en/commentaries/168/charles-simeons-horae-homileticae/genesis/3/15.

Sweet, Leonard, and Frank Viola. *Jesus Manifesto: Restoring the Supremacy and Sovreignty of Jesus Christ*. Nashville: Nelson, 2010.

Tolkien, J. R. R. *On Fairy Stories*. New York: HarperCollins, 2008.

———. *Tree and Leaf: Including* "Mythopoeia" *and* "The Homecoming of Beorhtnoth." Hammersmith. London: HarperCollins, 2001.

———. *Tolkien on Fairy-Stories*. Expanded ed. with commentary and notes. Edited by Verlyn Flieger and Douglas A. Anderson. London: HarperCollins, 2014.

Vanauken, Sheldon. *A Severe Mercy*. New York, NY: Harper, 1977.

Virgil. *The Aeneid*. Translated by W. F. Jackson Knight. Harmondsworth, London: Penguin, 1958.

Voth, Jeff. *Why Lewis? Seven Reasons Why C. S. Lewis Is the Second Most Influential Author in Modern Christian History*. Eugene, OR: Wipf and Stock, 2021.

Waltke, Bruce K. *Genesis: A Commentary*. Grand Rapids: Zondervan, 2001.

Wright, N. T. *The Day the Revolution Began*. New York: HarperCollins, 2016.

———, and Michael F. Bird. *The New Testament in Its World*. Grand Rapids: Zondervan, 2019.

CPSIA information can be obtained
at www.ICGtesting.com
Printed in the USA
BVHW090341201022
649851BV00004B/5